Shadows of My Past

Marcey Oliver

authorHOUSE®

AuthorHouse™ UK Ltd.
500 Avebury Boulevard
Central Milton Keynes, MK9 2BE
www.authorhouse.co.uk
Phone: 08001974150

First published by AuthorHouse   9/27/2012
Rev. 10/10/2012
ISBN: 978-1-4520-8972-0 (sc)
ISBN: 978-1-4520-8973-7 (hc)
ISBN: 978-1-4520-8974-4 (e)

Library of Congress Control Number: 2010915706

This book is printed on acid-free paper.

SHADOWS OF MY PAST

In the dimness
Of the twilight of my life,
I relive the happiness,
The muted pain and strife,
From the shadows of my past.

Gone is my youth,
Once filled with vibrant euphoria,
Due to visions and goals
And planning for the days ahead.

Kindergarten, Grade School
And higher learning,
To understand the vortex of the Whirlpool
Spinning in the world around me.

To relate to all the things with meaning,
And decide what path was best for me.
Of love once cherished, and then lost,
The eternal, the emotional,
Deep in the recesses of my heart.

The love and commitment of a love
That shone for all to see,
But snuffed out by death,
Still a mystery.

Then from the shadows,
And from the past,
True love was resurrected,
Sweeter on the second round,
A gift from God,
You are mine, you have always been mine,
He keeps drumming in my ear.

And from my past,
The dimness has a sunlit hue,
As I create new memories.
From the shadows of my past.

Marcey/2009

1
FAMILY

My name is Marcey, and I was born on an island, a very small island in the Caribbean, which was, at that time, a colony of Great Britain. To me, this was a huge place, and I could not imagine anywhere larger or more beautiful, with sunshine, warmth, and beautiful beaches. I am the oldest of the five children born to my parents

I am a mixture of many ethnicities. On my paternal side, I am Scottish, Portuguese, Jewish, and African. On my maternal side, I am Scottish, English, Irish, and African; that is all that I know of. My mother was a postmistress who was transferred to several post offices throughout the island. My father was an accountant at a very large and prosperous sugar cane plantation—the sugar made from that sugar cane was shipped to England, as was all other produce from the island.

My mother's family were all academics. My grandparents were both school principals. My aunts were teachers, pharmacists, nurses, university professors, a postmistress, and accountants. There were six aunts and one uncle, who died at birth. My aunts were all accomplished musicians; they played the guitar, the violin, and the piano. My mother played all instruments. My maternal grandparents had a lot of land that was chiefly used for raising goats, and my grandfather gave a goat to each of his grandchildren. My father's family were business people. My paternal grandfather was an exporter of spices and skins, and others in the family were nurses, accountants, managers, and housewives. There were five aunts, one who died at age five, and two uncles. My paternal grandparents also had a lot of land and animals, primarily dairy cattle, and to each of his grandchildren my grandfather gave a calf. My paternal grandmother stayed at home. She was an accomplished violinist and such a lady. I loved all my grandparents.

My roots are on the island of Jamaica and I am very proud of my heritage.

I have three brothers and one sister. My oldest brother attended a university in the United States, where he studied economics. My second oldest brother was a businessman; my youngest brother was a steam engineer and a millwright. My sister, now retired, was the manager of personnel at the company where she worked, and I have a bachelor of social work degree and was a career consultant for the company for which I worked.

The early days of my life were idyllic, and I would never change anything that happened in my life. My mother stayed at home, except when the post office called her out because they were short, and they needed her help. Our home had a cook, a housemaid, and a nursemaid for us kids. I had my own nursemaid for a while—her name was Sally, and whenever I went to visit my paternal grandparents Sally always came to see me. She called me "Miss Marcey." I have not seen her now for many years, as I heard that she went overseas to live.

One of my earliest recollections involves Sally. At the time we lived about ten miles or so from the nearest town in the parish in a great big house—at least it appeared that way to me. I later found out that it was haunted, and I cannot for the life of me understand why my parents bought it and went to live there; perhaps because it was closer to where my father worked. Once when I was four years old, my parents were away, and Sally's boyfriend, Johnny, came over to see her. He had a machete that he always carried, as he worked on a sugar plantation cutting sugar cane that was taken to the sugar estates to be made into sugar for mostly export As they were talking, he used the back of his machete to make little marks on a big guangu tree on our property. I ran up to them just as he swung the machete backward, and I got the sharp edge of the machete across my forehead, almost into my eyes. I remember the panic as Sally took me and laid me on the patio behind our house. I was bleeding profusely, and I remember that my brother kissed me because he thought I was going to die.

The telephones, then, were antiquated. They looked like huge boxes attached to the wall with a mouthpiece, a removable hand held receiver on one side and a little handle that was turned to make the number of rings for the person you were calling. It appeared to be a chore just to use it.

My parents were contacted and they were home in a jiffy. At the time, my father had a truck, so I was taken to the hospital in a truck. I was stitched up, and sent back home. It has been said that the accident slightly affected my eyes, and I had to wear glasses—those horrible old fashioned turtle shell glasses that I really hated.

My sister and second brother were born in this house. We were told that the "airplane" brought them, and we had to go to Mrs. Annie for cookies before the babies arrived each time. I could never understand why they were not hurt by the rocks when they were dropped from the plane. Many questions were asked as I wanted to know why the babies were never harmed, being dropped from an airplane on big rocks on the ground. I had to believe that the airplane brought the baby, because then, there were not many planes flying overhead, but it appeared that one always flew over when a new baby was born in my family. Major lessons were learned later when my mother told me a little about the facts of life.. We were all born at home, and each one was delivered by the same midwife. I believe she is still alive. She got a lot of business from the paternal side of my family, as she also delivered several of my cousins.

Christmastime was wonderful. Our first Christmas tree, as far as I can remember, was a branch of the willow tree that grew by the seaside—we lived by the ocean. It was wispy and droopy, but it was our tree. We trimmed it with crepe paper and perhaps one string of "pepper lights" as the indoor Christmas tree lights were called then. Gifts were sparse—one tricycle for all of us, a doll for me, and I don't know what the others got—it was not my concern. Santa Claus, or Father Christmas, as we called him then, came through the keyhole, and he could not come in if we were not asleep. I chanced staying awake once, and got nothing for Christmas. Santa Claus did not put gifts under the tree until we were much older. Before that, our gifts were put on our pillows above our heads as we slept. It was such a delight as we danced around, enjoying the gifts we got and taking care not to break anything.

Every Christmas we went to our grandparents' home for Christmas dinner with the entire family—aunts, uncles, cousins, and family friends. The veranda that circled the two sides and the front of the house was set up with long tables for the adults and smaller tables for the children. There was always a turkey, ham, roast beef, and a whole suckling pig with a potato in its mouth—the table was laden with food. I hated that pig. It scared me so much that I could not sleep, and I hated the dark. The turkeys patrolled the yard and chased us when we went out. We had to get them locked up,

3

especially the tom, who eventually landed on the Christmas table as our dinner. Turkey is not my most favorite meal, but I will eat it when it is fresh from the oven and served for dinner.

When I was four, my parents, in their infinite wisdom, sent me to stay with one of my grandaunts on the farm on another part of the island. I hated it there. My aunt Greta, who was my grandmother's sister, was mean, or so I thought. She locked me in the bedroom while she went out, and I never knew the reason. I was never a rude child or gave any trouble. My cousin Maddy was also at the farm, but she was older and therefore fared better than I did.

Then, there was the day the white miserable cow chased me. I was but a fluff of a thing. I had followed Aunt Greta across the commons to go to see the king and queen of England, who were visiting the island. My aunt told me that I couldn't come, so I went back to the farm and tried to climb over the gate. Betsy, the cow, who was nursing her calf, did not like me one bit, so she chased me. Thank goodness for my granduncle Art, who pulled me over the gate to safety. I hated Betsy—I hate all cows; they have no sense, yet I did grow up around them.

The home on the farm was the childhood home of my paternal grandmother. Her father was from Scotland, and her mother was an islander. I was told that she was a descendant of the queen of Sheba, but I have never been interested to find out if this was true. There was a lot of land on the farm that was later bought by the Bauxite Company. The house and the family cemetery are still there on the farmland. I could hardly wait for my parents to take me home; nothing would make me stay.

My security was short-lived; I went from the frying pan into the fire. I was now sent to live with my mother's sister, Lizzy, as it was time for me to learn what school was all about. For goodness sake, I was only four years and already a genius—what else was there to learn? If I thought Aunt Greta was the Wicked Witch of the West, I don't know what Aunt Lizzy was. She was the principal of a school in a rural area, about ten miles or so from the nearest town, and the capital of the parish, as each parish had a capital city or town. To get to her place, one had to pass the home of my maternal grandparents, and I loved going to see my grandparents as it was easier to see them when I went to stay with Aunt Lizzy.

Aunt Lizzy was cross, and apart from that being a part of her personality, I believe she took her responsibility seriously as she was now a guardian of her sister's child.—She did not allow me to play with any of the children in the school, as they were not good enough, so I tried to teach the ABC's to the trees—this has stuck with me throughout the years. I was afraid of Aunt Lizzy. She locked me in her room if I peed her bed. I wonder why I did that; I think she scared it out of me. My sister, brothers and cousins on my maternal side, all had our stint with Aunt Lizzy. My grandparents told my parents to take me home because Aunt Lizzy spanked a lot. I remember she had a yard boy who stole the marbles from her checker set, but he said that I'd given them to him. I never touched the sacred marbles, but I got a licking because I said I did not give the marbles to him. I cried so hard that I threw up in her face basin. That made me happy. My uncle Art died when I was with her, and I was really sad. My parents brought me home then.

My parents, by this time, had sold their house in the country and bought another house in the town, because of my father's transfer in his job. I was now six years. I was sick, and I had to be rushed to the hospital with appendicitis. Today, I have a scar that appears to be a scorpion carved in my stomach. I have no idea why this cut was so large. I guess surgeons had not completely honed in on their skills at that time. .

2

SCHOOL

I grew up with mostly dogs as pets, as my mother did not like cats due to an unfortunate experience she encountered. There was always a dog in our family. I loved puppies, so I treated them as children. My recollection of the first dog I saw was a dog we called Chiwey. She was a black collie, and she had several puppies. I don't remember when we no longer had her, because I was not always at home. Then there was Laddie, then Bumstead, then Rover—these are the ones I remember. My sister and I later sneaked a kitten into our home, and when it was older, we watched as this cat had four kittens. That was an experience I have never forgotten. I also grew up with chickens and other animals, as my grandparents had properties that had cows, goats, horses, donkeys, and other farm animals.

I did not have one specific pet, just the puppies when my parents brought a dog home. I was never attached to any one thing. My cousin and I fed milk to baby goats from a bottle with a nipple, because the mother would not feed it. We both nursed chickens back to health when we thought they had the "pip" (a disease that caused scales or crust on their tongues) and could not pick up their food, which was ground kernels of corn. We would also make a racket by beating pots and pans with a spoon over the chickens' heads if we thought they were sick and dying. This usually revived them. I wonder why?

As a child, I did not have many toys, because I was always outside. However, my dolls were important. I had one doll that my parents bought and several that were handmade. When I was ten or eleven, my friend Maud, who lived next door, sewed clothes for my dolls. She was an excellent seamstress at that young age.

Age six was a tumultuous year for me. I must have been a horrible child, because it was then that I was shipped off to boarding school— Navaho's Secondary School, which I hated—in the middle of the island. I lived by the ocean. My parents' friends had a daughter, Nancy Nicks, who also went there; she was not the swiftest of the pack. Then there was Leonard Darrow. He looked like Tubby Tompkins from the *Little Lulu* comics and had a mouth like Iggy Inch also from the Little Lulu Comics, and although these characters were not "cry babies" I associated Leonard with them. That kid was always crying, and he was not the best-looking, with his protruding belly in his short pants. *Oh, Lord*, I thought, *my parents must hate me*, and even at my tender age, I vowed that I would never send any of my children to a boarding school. Most of all, I made a vow that I would never have a child like Leonard Darrow.

Except for Sheila Cooks, I have never seen anyone from my boarding school days, .She, however, was older than I was. If there's anything I want to block from my mind about my childhood, it is boarding school days. Breakfast was one roll with margarine and a cup of hot chocolate. Noon meal was "flour stew" on rice when eaten, felt as though it had rocks from where it was harvested, and then mixed with sardines. Rice then was sold by weight or by the pound, the metric system of that day. It was not properly cleaned, unlike the packaged long grain or short grain rice sold in the supermarket today. My parents paid extra so I could have some milk. Supper was one roll again with margarine and a glass of lemonade. In later life, when I tried to gain weight, I could not move from ninety-eight pounds because my body was set at the starvation mode.

Imagine: I went to Navaho's for four years. My parents had to bribe me with tons of new clothing to get me to go back, and on top of that, every month, a basket of goodies came by bus for me. On those occasions, I had a lot of friends who were hungry and starved also. When I was young, children were to be "seen and not heard," so no one complained about the conditions at school. On my first night home from school at the end of each term, I got sick because I tried to eat everything in sight.

When I learned how to read, I became a bookworm. I joined the public library and read fairy tales by Hans Christian Andersen and Grimm's Fairy Tales. The story about Falada the horse became a favorite fairy tale. I then moved on to reading about Scotland and the lairds of the castles. I liked the travelogue of the different castles and Highlands of Scotland. I got in a lot of trouble from my parents, because when the lights were to be out for bed, I would read with a flashlight. Their predictions that I would ruin my eyes, and would have to wear glasses later in life, came true, as I now wear glasses.

I grew apart from my siblings, because I was never home. I started piano lessons at six years old while at Navaho's. I did get a scholarship for tuition for all the years I was there. I wish it had been for food also. My pocket money was five shillings, as that was the currency then, and that was to buy treats at homework time—Bulla which was a sweet round cake or Gratto, which was a local flatbread and to this very day I hate those things. There was no "aerated water," as pop was called then, or anything to wash it down. Then there were mint balls and paradise plums that left ridges in the roof of your mouth if you kept it there for any amount of time, which also made your tongue sore Although, as a child, these treats were good, I soon learned to associate them with pain and sores, and I hate them to this very day; We could not write to tell our parents anything because our letters were censored, in the event we told our parents just how much we hated boarding school, and the reasons why we did. During one school year, some of us became ill with the chicken pox, and had to be quarantined until we got over it. I turned ten in January, and I begged my parents not to send me back. I was a bright little thing. Navaho's taught me well, as I was to have taken my junior Cambridge when I left, then senior Cambridge two years later. These were British education standard exams, which I would not be able to compare to the education standards of today, as a lot has changed and then what? Graduate from high school at age twelve? I don't think so. My parents finally took me out of boarding school.

My aunt and uncle had inherited a business and wanted to sell, so my parents bought the business, moved there, and rented out our house. This was good, as I could now eat all the candies I wanted, all the good imported ones that were wrapped in paper, mostly toffees Our home was now above the place of business; it had six bedrooms. My mother invited her sister to move down from the capital city to live with us. She had a pharmacy there that was not doing so well, so she came, much to my father's chagrin. She was divorced, and was the mother of two children that she brought with her, now, we had two cousins to deal with on a daily basis.

I now went to another private school as a day student for ages ten and eleven, and I enjoyed that, as I could now live at home with my parents. As kids, my cousins and I spent many happy and wonderful holidays when we all met at my paternal grandparents for holidays. They only lived about three miles away on the family property, called Haven Dew. On this property, my grandfather had a lot of seville orange trees that he grafted with other species of oranges and grapefruits to get the best grapefruits and navel oranges. Some trees were off limits to us, but as kids, we didn't listen. My cousin Zickle and I ate so many oranges one day that I got so sick, I wished I would have died. Grandpa knew what we had done. I bet I am the only grandchild who got a spanking from him. We had all gone up to spend the evening with them. My parents rode bikes. My brother and I were left to spend the night. I did not want to stay—I hated the nights there in the lamp light as the flickering flame cast a lot of shadows that were scary, and as kids, we had heard so many stories about ghosts from the people that worked in our homes, that I was almost petrified of the dark, as ghosts came out at nights. So, I walked down to the gate, climbed through, and began walking with the people who were walking to town. "Shaggy," a man that my father grew up with and with whom he went bird shooting and fishing, was supposed to have come back for my brother and me. He saw me, put me on his bike, and took me home to my parents who did not question my arrival, as that was the plan. Shaggy was to come back to take both my brother and myself home – they probably thought that my brother wanted to stay with my grandparents that is why he did not come home with me, besides, there were no telephones in either of our homes to check.

Well the next morning, my grandfather was at our home bright and early. I got a good talking to and a few slaps. In retrospect, I don't know what I was thinking. I could have been kidnapped. I was lucky the people knew "Mass Georgie" and "Miss Ada," so they took care of me. Perhaps that experience is why I was so particular in knowing where my own children were when they were younger.

I collected stamps when I was a child; this was something I loved to do. I also collected marbles. Today, I do not know where these things are. I had four siblings, and they seemed to love my collections.

Yes, college was where I met Lewis Hanna. I don't know who had the crush, but when he wrote me and told me that he was going to kiss me that particular evening, I ran home and never spoke to him again. Before that, we were good friends—our families exchanged visits. We went to Sunday school together. He even gave me a ring that I gave to my mother, as I was so embarrassed to have it. Lewis Hanna made a mistake in trying to show a special interest in me. I was not ready for that, so I never spoke to him again, neither did I see him after I left for high school in the capital. Maud, Naomi, Brad, Tim, Leonard, Mark, Julie, and Martha—all friends—went for walks together to the little bridge and big bridge; lots of fun. When

I see the area now, I don't know how we never got killed. Perhaps it was because there were not many cars on the roads in those days. When we were younger, at four in the afternoon, we had to be showered and dressed before my parents came home. We would be taken for a walk before dinner, and then it would be bedtime. When we got older, it was the same, except we could go for walks on our own; hence, big bridge and little bridge.

I had to take the island scholarship exams, as told by my school. I had to go to the capital with my dad. I loved that. I always loved going places with my dad. I remember one particular movie, *Moby Dick*, about a big whale, which was, very scary, but my Dad would protect me. Anyway, I did the exam, although I did not study. I applied to high school and did not have to take the entrance examinations because I was in the first one hundred students who did very well on their scholarship exams. I wished that I had studied, as I might have gotten a scholarship, but it was good, as I did not have to take another trip to the capital. I was still age eleven. On the island, the school year started in January and ended in December. I believe it has since changed. So in January, just before I turned twelve years old, I started at an all-girls high school. I was now living in the city and boarding again with my aunt, one of my mother's sisters, and her family—cousins that I did not know as well as my cousins on my father's side of the family. My father also boarded with them, as he was wooed by another company in the capital to work with them. At least I had a part of my family there.

Somehow, some of my freedoms were now kept under wraps as now living with my aunt, I could not go to the movies with my friends from school as I would have liked. I felt stifled. My mother's family, who were all Anglicans originally, all seemed to be overly religious and moved toward the Church of God and the Pentecostal movements, except my mother, who was now looked upon as a sinner and a *worldlian*, as they called it. I had gone to church with my own family on Sunday mornings and Sunday school in the evenings, but I was now going to Sunday school from 9:00 to 10:00 AM and to church from 10:00 AM to noon, and then sometimes church again from 7:00 to 9:00 PM. I did not like that one bit. A couple times my dad got talked into going. My brother came up to the capital to go to high school when he was old enough, at age twelve and came to board with my aunt for a short while.

Every morning there was worship before breakfast and before we went anywhere. My first year of high school went okay. I had to put up with moods of my cousins, rules and regulations in the home of my aunt, and religion, that stifled what I wanted to do, which was to go to a movie with my friends, reading movie magazines, and just the normal things kids of my age would want to do. I remember getting in trouble from my uncle for buying a movie magazine with my pocket money. I did, however, buy a lot of bubble gum to get the cards of movie stars, which I saved and traded. I suppose life was good because I did not know any better. I continued throughout the years with my piano lessons. I wanted to take ballet lessons but could not. I played tennis only for sports at school and actually hated gym classes. My dad and my brother moved to board with one of his sisters; now I was on my own. My mother wanted to move to the capital also, but she had the business to take care of and three other children who were under high school age. My father went home as often as he could. This separation, I learned later, was not good for our family or for my parents' marriage. My mother, however, was determined to hold everything together.

She sold the business at a loss and with oodles of monies owed to them and moved to the capital. Now, finally, we could all live together again. I was thirteen. I believe my moving during early childhood led to my search for trust. I don't blame my parents for sending me to all the people in our family that I stayed with when I was young. Perhaps it was not for long periods of time, but when I was a child, one day was an eternity, especially when my mother's love was absent in my life. I searched for love and acceptance from the adults to whom my parent entrusted me, but it was not always there. This really messed with my belief system, which was carried throughout my life. I wanted to love, I wanted to trust, and when I thought I had found love and I truly trusted, that trust was shattered, and I had to start all over again.

It was wonderful having, and living with my mother continuously. For the first time in all my life, I finally got to live with her, at home, and I knew that I was not going to be sent off anywhere else. If I was to go anywhere, it would be my decision, and it would be for holidays only.

The best years of my young life were spent with my paternal cousins. My father's oldest sister was like a second mother to me, and she is by far my most favorite aunt. Zickle, her youngest daughter, and I were the same age, so we spent a lot of time growing up together. We met just about every summer holiday at Haven Dew, the home of my grandparents, or at her parents' home, wherever her father worked as an overseer of a sugar cane plantation. Her older siblings were my favourite cousins. Their experiences were like mine. They, too, were sent to stay with other relatives—that

11

was the order of the day. Her oldest sister is my favorite of all my cousins. I have to say that although Zickle is my cousin, she became my own sister, so that rules out the word cousin. I was really not very close to my own siblings; that came later. Zickle finally came to the capital to stay at another of my father's sister's house to continue high school. I was so happy living with my own family. Zickle and I used to meet to go to the movie matinee almost every Saturday afternoon. Zickle, however, got so homesick that she went back home to her parents to finish her education. I had made friends in high school but had some restrictions where parties were concerned—who and where—so I really did not bother to pursue this avenue, I was not that interested.

My mother got invited to go to a Pentecostal church because some missionaries from overseas were coming, so she took me with her. The proceedings were so emotional; it really made an impression on my sixteen-year-old, innocent psyche. I continued to go there, against my mother's better judgment. I really thought I was doing the right thing—they preached going against what your parents said, to follow God, and told of all the bad things that could happen if you refused to follow God, and so on. I felt I should have known better, but I was actually afraid, so I kept going for four years. Then I began to see the flaws. Everything that was normal and good and that was enjoyable was bad in the eyes of the church. I began to grow up and grow past all these narrow teachings. I was a realist and could not feel what I saw some people feeling. I felt that if the emotions they expressed were true, then it would also happen to me, and it did not, and I was not about to pretend. I went back to my own religion as an Anglican. After I left the Pentecostal church that I had attended, I was searching for something. I wanted traditions on how to serve God. The members of the Pentecostal church tried to get me back—they said I was a "backslider." I suppose I was, but I had outgrown them, and I was not going back. I will worship God according to my own beliefs.

I loved my high school years. I had lots of fun. The boys at our "brother" school, just next door to us, were so funny and tried to get our attention. I particularly liked going to school championships, when all the boys' schools competed against each other in track-and-field and also at soccer championships. Boys were so funny, but there were some very funny girls, also—lots of laughter and classroom pranks on the teachers, which resulted in detentions for the perpetrators. I graduated from high school in December 1957 after I sat for my final exams. I was seventeen years old. In January 1958 I returned to high school to await the results of my final exams which came out in March of that year. Our exams (The Senior Cambridge Exams) were designed by the British, and marked in England as our education system was British. With my success, I then completed my three month term in high school, and went on to commercial college. I did not really like it there and did not complete the course. I got my first job with a bottling company, where I stayed for four months; then I went on to one of the radio stations. I worked for three months as a stenographer with what I had learned at commercial college—and hated it. I requested a transfer to the accounting department to be trained as an accounting-machine operator. I was nineteen. I loved my job. I billed clients for time and commercials they put on the radio. During that time, I had applied to a university in Scotland to get a degree in home economics/dietetics but chose not to go. I decided that I did not want to leave home—I did not know where I was going in Scotland or what I would encounter. Besides, I knew no one there.

There were a couple boys that came around—Barry and Aaron and others. I had a schoolgirl crush on Edward London while in school. Although I never, ever spoke to him, there are a couple of trees on my grandparents' property on which I had carved his name. I spent eighteen months at the radio station. I was liked by Nigel Williams, Leonard Johnson, and perhaps others. I know this, because they told me so. Nigel attended my twenty-first birthday party, organized by my parents. I had no particular interest in Nigel. I have forgotten my first simple kiss at age nineteen, but I have not forgotten my first proposal of marriage at age sixteen. That was the most devastating thing that happened to me. I was still in high school and paid no particular interest to Raymond. I had never even held his hand, which was a big deal. I never spoke to him again because I was so embarrassed at his interest in me, especially when I had to tell him that I had no interest in him. I heard that he later became a professor at the university. Then there was Robert, who is now a scholar at the university. Leonard Johnson pursued me and to whom I showed a little interest. He went overseas to university to study engineering. My second marriage proposal. There was no response from me at his proposal. He wrote many letters until I got a phone call from a girl telling me that she was Leonard Johnson's fiancée. I asked myself, who else was he writing to? That was the end of that friendship, as I was not about to find out.

3
WORK, FRIENDSHIPS, FALLING IN LOVE, AND HEARTACHE

At age twenty-one I started work at the Light and Power office of the Public Service Company, as a ledger clerk. I loved my job. I liked anything to do with figures. I suppose in that respect, I followed in my father's footsteps. He was an accountant and is now the chief paymaster at the company for which he works. He received many accolades from overseas for his accuracy. After being a ledger clerk, I requested a transfer to the bookkeeping-machine department, where I would bill customers for the amount of electricity they used. I really loved my job but not the supervisor—she was miserable. I was the youngest employee and the only single person on her staff, so she felt she had the upper hand and tried to keep me under control. It did not work, because then I rebelled.

Janet and Cara became my closest friends. I had been playing badminton for years at my old place of employment, and I still played after I left. So, I now invited my Light and Power friends to play against my old team. Janet, Cara, Fiona, and I would always go to the matinee movie after work on Fridays, which was a lot of fun. Cara's father would pick us up and take us to our respective homes.

It was the summer of 1962 when Janet invited Frederick Dempster, an auditor with a noted auditing firm, to join us on our weekly Friday trek to the matinee—I think it was to see an Elvis Presley flick about a mundane love affair and singing. I was invited to Cara's home the following night to play a game called Pokeno, and Frederick was to bring a couple friends from the Old Boys Football Club with him. I was not going to attend, but Cara and Janet were determined that I should, so Mr. and Mrs. Mac, Cara's parents, came to pick me up. Frederick turned up with Deiter Chabot and Larry Winston They were very tall men; Frederick was the shortest of the three. Their presence filled Mrs. Mac's kitchen, where we were to play this game. They were pretty noisy, especially Deiter who appeared to be the jester of the group. We played this game for pennies; it was my first introduction to gambling.

We were joined by Cara's parents, her brother, Paul, and his wife, Wendy. We had so much fun playing for pennies that everyone wanted to steal the "penny pot." We played well into the night, laughing, talking, and teasing. I had never had so much fun—Deiter Chabot was such a funny person. Frederick, Deiter and Larry, took Janet and me home, and Cara came along with us for the ride. I lived the farthest away, so I was taken home first. There were six of us packed into a Volkswagen Beetle, it was a little cramped, but we had a lot of fun. We then played Pokeno often at each other's houses, as this game became the order of the day. We even invited other friends to join us. We all had a lot of fun, and that entailed a lot of teasing and laughter. Special friendships were established, and we would also go to the drive-in movie as a group. Larry dropped out of the group, as he was now engaged to someone else.

Another game we played was a very significant one called "Truth or Consequences." We girls thought it was a smart idea to find out about these young men, which we could do by playing this game, and by then, another young man had come on the scene—his name was Donald Leong. Well, we did find out a lot, and I believe they did tell us the truth. Some special attractions were formed: Frederick was interested in Janet, and Donald was interested in Cara.

Deiter and I had no connection; he had a girlfriend, Kitty. Perhaps to some degree, there was Leonard for me—before I got the call from the girl telling me she was his fiancée. I did not love Leonard; Janet made more of that friendship than I did. We now attended several parties as a group, danced, and had a lot of fun. Laughter was the order of the day, as these guys were certainly funny.

It was November 6ʼ and it was Deiter's birthday. We were all invited to attend his birthday party. Janet and I had a badminton competition match to play at one of the hotels, so we arrived late. We got a ride to the party with Roger Whalen, another friend who played Pokeno with us. This was a very nice party. Deiter's girlfriend was there, and so was Larry's girlfriend—a girl I knew from my old hometown. I could tell that Deiter's girlfriend did not like Cara. Poor Cara—she was an innocent victim of this dislike. We attended a lot of parties and danced a lot.

For New Year's Eve 1962, Janet organized a party at her house. I attended. The girls brought food, and the guys brought the drinks, which mostly consisted of very little alcohol. Donald Leong, who now joined us regularly, was there. So were Cara, Frederick, and Deiter, who brought Kitty and who for some reason was not a very happy camper—there appeared to be some fussing and tension between her and Deiter. My brother and my sister and her boyfriend were all in attendance.

During the course of the night, Deiter asked me to dance with him. Mr. Acker Bilk's record was on the stereo. He was playing away on his clarinet, and the music he played was for easy listening, and it was really soothing. Deiter was such a great dancer. We danced for the entire side of an LP record. I don't know what happened, but something did. He was shaking, and so was I. There were some emotions that I had never felt before and that I tried to downplay, but I could not help feeling the magic of the moment. I put the experience out of my mind, as I dared not entertain any thoughts. I am a very serious person, and I did not take this lightly. Until then, I had no designs on Deiter Chabot. That weekend, my mind gravitated toward him, but because of the way girls were supposed to behave, I would have never phoned him. How would I see him again? Something happened to me, and I did not know what or how to contain it. I said nothing to Janet or Cara—or to anyone, for that matter.

New Year's Day was spent as per normal, but on January 2, 1963, the phone rang at work, and it was Deiter. My heart was about to fall from my chest. I could hardly talk to him, because I was shaking. After that, the calls became numerous, and I would always shake. Janet, Frederick, Cara, Larry, Deiter and I went to the drive-in, and somehow, it was different. I was attracted to Deiter and him to me, and he told me so. I was extremely aware of his presence and his eyes on me.

He leaned across and kissed me in my ear, and my heart stopped beating. I reminded him of Kitty, and he said he had broken up with her. Much later, I became more receptive to his advances, and when our lips met for the first time, my body went limp as my heart stopped beating. We became an item—the last set to become a couple. He phoned me every morning and every night and came over as often as he could, when he could get his father's car. I was truly happy and so very much in love with him—1963 was a very happy year. I spent Christmas with him and was invited to dinner with his family. The extent of this passionate love was relegated to kissing, and I thought I was going to die each time our lips connected. I just wanted to go on kissing forever. My body shook with emotion, and so did his as he told me that he loved me. He was such a gentleman.

We saw each other as often as we could, and we continued to go out as a group. It was a good year. On New Year's Eve 1963, it was pouring rain. Deiter and I did not see each other. He said he could not come over, but I believe he did go out to a party somewhere, as when I called his house, I was told that he was not at home. He came over on my birthday, January 9th and we went out, and I think 1964 started out all right.

This was the year that Janet got sick—I believe it was asthma—in about March or April. We went to see her. Something was wrong. Deiter sat on the veranda by himself, and he appeared to be a little morose. I asked if I could sit with him, and the response I got was unlike him: "Suit yourself." I thought it was very rude and being as sensitive as I was, I was really hurt, so I left him and went back inside. I had never seen this side of him—he was always talkative and funny. I felt he had no right to speak to me in that manner. I was devastated and questioned his lack of respect. I would not under any circumstances speak to him like that. Donald Leong drove, so we went with him to get dropped off at home.

I did not want Deiter to take me to my door, so I walked in alone. The normal procedure was he would have my key, he would walk me to my door, we have a few kisses, and he would then open my door and see me safely in. Then he'd return my key and walk back to his car and be on his way home. Because of the above mentioned misunderstanding, it appeared that our friendship was never the same. He hardly called, which made me really angry. Perhaps there was some method to his madness, but I could not see it at the time. My anger turned to one of sorrow and bewilderment. I hardly saw him, and I did not know the reason why.

I learned that he was now making plans to go overseas to attend university. When the time came for him to leave, he came over to my house to tell me good-bye. Donald Leong came with him. My heart was breaking as he kissed me, and it finally broke when I asked him, "Deiter, what do you want me to do? Wait or what?" And he told me, "I will write." He further said, "Let me look at this house, as I will never see this for another four years." He said that he would phone me the following morning before he left for the airport, but he never phoned. Had I wasted all this time loving someone who did not really love me or care? I said to myself, "Okay, I will wait for his letter. Let me see what he writes to tell me."

I waited an eternity—actually, three weeks—for one page, which told me exactly nothing. I had not asked him to marry me; I just wanted some sort of security in a friendship, and to know if he wanted me to wait on him until he completed his university, and what would happen next. I was devastated again. My parents, unbeknown to me, were watching this episode play out. They saw my hurt. I never could confide in them. I would take to my bed and cry myself to sleep. I must have had rocks in my head to allow myself to be so affected, but I was in love. If anyone had asked me about a broken heart, I would have had lots to tell, but I tried to hide it from my parents. I told them nothing, but parents know when something is not going right with their children. I guess this experience of my own broken heart was training for later on in my life on how to help my own children when they had broken hearts.

I received a second letter from Deiter a few months later, but it was a Christmas card, and it was no better than the first. In the meantime, I kept writing to him and asking questions that were never answered. He had said that he was going to St. Paul Minneapolis for a little holiday. Other people got letters, which really ate away at my confidence and my self-esteem. I wondered what had I done that was so wrong. Cara received several letters from Donald Leong, chock-full of things a girl would want to hear from the person who she believed was her boyfriend, but not me. I wrote every week because I thought Deiter must be lonesome, so I would keep him company. He never replied.

I sent him a birthday card and a gift. I sent him a Christmas card and a gift. I did not need to get anything in return; I just loved to share things with him. I was devastated, however, when he didn't respond. Thank God for Frederick and Cara, they were always there to listen and to comfort me in my sadness. I am sure they thought I was going to lose my mind. I felt like every ounce of energy was taken away from me, and my body felt empty and was devoid of emotion, except for tears—I did not know I had that many.

Cara and I chummed around a lot. My father had given me a car that we named the "May Reach, (as I was never sure it would get us to our destination), so I went over to Cara's house a lot and brought her over to mine. We went over to see Mr. and Mrs. Chabot a lot, too. I used to visit and talk with them. I also talked to Deiter's brothers. They were very nice people, and I loved them. It was now Christmastime. This time of the year meant so much to me. Deiter and I had started a friendship then. I loved Christmas, because he was a part of my life. I loved the carols; I just loved the season. I was aching inside, until I went to see his parents and saw Kitty there. That just simply unnerved me. Had he been writing her? Why was she there? Had he been seeing her while he was seeing me? I did see him one night, taking her home, but I sort of pushed that aside, as he was seeing me at the time. Now, I realized that I had better recall that thought.

I had never been to a psychic before, but Cara and I went, even though I was extremely scared. I was just waiting for the psychic to tell me that I was going to die or something, and that might have been a good thing. She put some tea leaves in a teacup with water, and then swished it around. She then showed me two L's in the bottom of the teacup, and I was scared to death. I wanted to see a "D." Could this L mean Leonard? Oh, Lord, no! I did not want to marry him. She went on to tell me that I was going to be engaged in a month that started with the letter J. I also would be married in a month that started with the letter J, and I was going to live in a country that used the dollar as their currency, and I was going to have four children. My husband was going to love me eternally—he would be generous, and I was going to be well off. There would be nowhere that I went that he would not know where I was, because he was going to follow me. I was really upset—there was no "D." The psychic also told me that there were two men crying at my doorstep, and that I should just walk over them. I had no idea what all this was, and because that was not what I had wanted to hear, I put it out of my mind and never thought about it again.

I continued to wait for a letter from Deiter. It had now been about eight to ten months of uncertainty, which started from the night on Janet's veranda and now had culminated in zero correspondence and indifference. I said, "I have had enough. I can't win or make someone love me if he doesn't. How much more do I need to understand?" I had been going up to his house to spend time with his parents, as that made me feel close to him. That was good, because they were wonderful parents. I even felt that his mother could tell how my heart was hurting. I felt that I had to save myself—how, I did not know. Going out with someone else was the farthest thing from my mind.

I decided not to write to Deiter anymore. I was no longer going to entertain him in my thoughts, and I did not want anyone else in my life. Lord knows, there were several who would have liked my attention, but I did not give them the time of day. I needed to put my life back together, and I had no idea of how I was going to accomplish this major feat.

My cousin came to the island with his new wife to meet the family. He brought a friend named Les with him, whom I met when I saw them all downtown in one of the department stores. They were all shopping; they came over, hugged me, and introduced me to Les. Then my cousin and his wife continued shopping and left me with Les. I was on my lunch break from work, so I did not have much time to chitchat, so I just said to him, "Welcome to the island, and I hope you have a good time." Then I darted off and left him, as I was on my way back to work. I never had another thought of this man I had just met and with whom I seemed to have been thrown.

Two days later, they all came over to my parents' house for the evening. The usual hors d'oeuvres and drinks were served. I was not interested in anything, but went through the motions as I was supposed to when there were guests in the house. I did not pay any particular attention to Les. When they were leaving, the usual hugs and kisses for family members were the order of the day. Les wanted to know if he could have a kiss also, so I obliged by kissing him on his forehead—until then, my lips had belonged to Deiter Chabot.

4
MEETING MY HUSBAND

On Christmas Eve 1964, Donna and Sam, my cousins, had a party for friends and family, and being family, we all had to go. I really did not want to go, but my parents dictated that I must. Les was there, and I found out later that he had anticipated my arrival. He never left my side. I was embarrassed, as everyone was watching what was happening. I approached one of my brothers and offered to pay him ten shillings, the currency then, to dance with me, so that I would not have to dance with Les. When it was time to go, I was happy to go home with my parents. The next morning, Les was on the phone, and I really did not know what to say to him. Later that day, the family and Les came over to my parents' house. We all went out to visit other family members and came back to my house for Christmas dinner. When the others were ready to go home, Les did not want to leave, so he asked if he could stay a little longer. I asked my parents, and they said they would take him home later, or I could drive him back, accompanied by my brother or my sister. Later, I thought to myself, *Let me see what type of person this man is.* I had already established that he was a communicator, and he wanted to talk with me.

Now, the roof on my parents' house was flat and was used as a patio. The front of the patio overlooked the avenue where we lived, and it was not very private. The back of the patio overlooked the carport, (garage) and was therefore more private. Deiter and I always sat towards the back of the patio, and the rest was open territory. Les and I went on the roof toward the front of my house and talked forever. He was really a very nice man, which I found out as soon as I gave him a chance and began talking and listening to him. I believe I asked him a zillion questions. I first told him that I had a boyfriend, but there was no commitment between us. Les listened and said not a word about Deiter. We just talked forever, and I was very comfortable in his company. I felt that I had known him for a very long time. I could ask him anything that I wanted, and he always gave me a truthful answer. There were no kisses, just talking. I was in control, and that felt strange. There was no emotional turmoil, and I loved his maturity.

He asked me to go to a movie. At first, I declined, but he asked me several times, and I finally said, "Okay, but the only reason I would go out with you is because you are my cousin's friend, and you are a guest of my family." Les did not go home that night—it was after 9:00 PM, and I did not want to drive him home at that time and return alone. He stayed at our house, and we made up the sofa for him to sleep on. I took him back to Donna and Sam's the next day. We all went over to their neighbors for lunch and a small party. Later that night, I went up to Cara's and told her all that had transpired. Until then, I had not been interested in Les.

It was now time for Les to leave Jamaica. Dennis, my cousin, and Marcia, his new wife, were going back to Canada, but Les had tickets to visit every other West Indian island—he often said he had a ticket as long as his arm. He did not want to leave the island; he wanted to stay to be with me. He asked me if he should go or stay. I said I did not care. In the meantime, I had asked Dennis about him, and I got a favorable review. I finally said to Les, "Stay if you like," so he did. He stayed over at Donna and Sam's. I still had not gone to the movie with him—or anywhere, for that matter.

He asked me to go out with him on New Year's Eve, to a hotel on the north coast. Four of my other cousins were going. He asked my parents to allow me to go with him. We all stayed at Haven Dew, my grandparents' home and property, three miles out of the nearest town.

New Year's Day was quiet. Les and I went for a walk. I took him all over my grandparents' property. I showed him the tree on which I'd carved the name of Edward London. I walked with him on the road to Merrywood and told him that when we were all kids, we used to walk with the helpers to where they milked the cows. My grandfather had a dairy cattle farm called Holland, and we went there also to watch them milk the cows. In those days, everything was done by hand, and I got several opportunities to do just that—and that had not been easy for me. I had milk, fresh from the cow, but I can't say that I liked that. We all had New Year's Day dinner with my grandparents.

We then went back to the capital and to our respective homes. Again, I went up to Cara and told her all that had transpired. I had no time to let anyone else know what was happening, as everything was happening so fast, and if I wanted to write anyone, whatever I had to say would have been after the fact anyway. But then, why bother? Deiter did not care what I did, as he did not even write or respond to any of my letters. My intent was now to move on with my life. I had to. My heart was still bruised, but I would try to get over it, and I never thought I was doing anything wrong or hurting anyone by going out with Les. I was the one who had been hurt—and was still hurting—but I found comfort in just talking to Les.

Les and I finally went to the movie. He asked me, "If you were to become engaged, what type of an engagement ring would you like?" I said, "I have no intention of marrying anyone, so what sort of a question is that? However, in the event that I was to become engaged, I would like a solitaire." I had no idea what a solitaire was, but I had heard that description. Les kissed me, and although this kiss did not evoke the same feelings that Deiter's kisses did, I soon put this experience behind me. I was the driver, so I took him home. The next evening, he wanted to come over to our house, so my aunt brought him over. He wanted to stay, and my parents said he could. He shared the bedroom with the boys, as there were three beds in that room. My oldest brother had left home for university the year before.

Les stayed at our home for the next two weeks. He would get up in the mornings and get a ride with us on our way to work. I would meet him for lunch, and then he would take a cab, drop me off at work, and continue home, where he would suntan on the patio on our roof. We would go out in the evenings to visit Cara and Janet. This was getting serious. He asked me to marry him again and again, and after much thought and hesitation, I said yes, because this friendship felt comfortable, and he was really a nice, honest man. I felt that I loved him enough to say yes. He asked my father for my hand in marriage. My father gave us both a lecture, reminding Les that I was an island girl, for whom he would be responsible. I really felt in control, and we got engaged.

Deep in my heart, someone named Deiter had bored a hole. I tried to patch it as best I could. He did not care—he never wrote, he had not told me that he loved me before he left, and certainly not now. I just knew that he did not care. Then, after months of no contact, he phoned me on my birthday—and I felt sick. I felt that I did not have to tell him anything because I felt that our friendship was over, because he hadn't written to me.

Taking into consideration the way he'd left me when he went to university, I felt that I was fighting a losing battle, and I was humiliated.

It was good to hear from him, although I was very nervous. He asked me if I still loved him. I knew I did, so I did say yes. Les was sitting at the dining room table when I took this call, and I was in the hallway. I also said to Deiter that I had something to tell him. He told me to write him "something different." I did not know what that meant. After the call, Les asked me if I had told Deiter anything as yet, and I said no. So, he made me write to Deiter right away. I did not want to, because I wanted to tell him in my own way why I had decided to get married. It was the fact that he'd left me, and I had found someone else that I loved and who loved me. I was now committed. Deiter had not told me on the phone that he loved me and that he wanted to marry me; he just asked me to write to him. Well, my letter was cut-and-dried: "Don't write; don't phone; I am engaged." I did not really like telling him like that, but I decided that I would write and tell him everything later, and he would understand—or so I thought

That Saturday, I received a letter from him. Oh, my God, I felt sick again. It was the letter I had waited on for six months and what I had wanted to hear for almost ten months. I was not looking for marriage; I just wanted comfort and the assurance of knowing that he loved me; that he really cared and that he wanted me to wait until he was finished at university.

Our letters crossed in the mail. His letter to me was finally full of all that I wanted to hear, and mine to him was not good at all. I had wanted to write him one more letter, in my time, to tell him that I was engaged to be married, but with Les' help, the letter I wrote was cut-and-dried and so much unlike me.

His letter told me more than I expected. "Dearest Marcey, it was so nice to hear your voice. I have really missed you. ... I have come to the realization that you are the only one in this world that can make me happy and make my life complete. I would like you to be my wife and to be the mother of my children. You have no idea just how much I really love you. ..." I felt every inch of the emotion that went into that letter. This was the man I had known so well, the man I loved so much.

My God, I'd really messed up this time. This was the man I had wanted to marry all along. I felt that someone had told him that I had been seeing Les and that he was only writing me because of that. I was afraid. I had already made a commitment to Les; besides, I'd written to tell

Deiter that he should not write or phone me; that I was engaged—I could not take that back. I also felt that if I did, he would not like me anyway. I had thought I would never see Deiter again. I remembered our parting and what he had said about "not seeing this house again for another four years." It was very hard for a while, because I truly felt that he was going to find an American girl or that he had found one and that was why he never wrote me. I was very scared.

I never wanted to hurt anyone; I never thought I was hurting anyone but myself—until I kept getting his letters. Then I sat down and penned to him the letter I had wanted to write: "I wanted to be your wife. I wanted to be the mother of your children. I loved you ..." and so on, and I was again hurting as I did this. I felt extremely sick, but as I had studied, people usually push the things that hurt them deep into the recesses of their souls and try to make the best of each situation. I just knew that I would never see Deiter again and that made it easier for me. After all, that is what he said when he left, and four years is a long time—a life sentence without knowing what was happening to my life. My astrological symbol is the goat—I am Capricorn—surefooted and never leaving things to chance. I love with all my heart and soul, and I had now kissed Les.

By this time, Les was back in Canada. If I had done as he wanted, I would have been married already, as he wanted to take me back. My response to that was, "Are you crazy?" We had to see the priest and fill out a form for marriage before he left, because it was protocol that he is here at least a few months before he could get a license to marry. It had to be announced in the church ahead of time, so if any one objected, he could state his objection. Les was a perfect gentleman. He left me as he had found me. I told him that I trusted him and that I knew he would never betray my trust by forcing me to do anything that I did not want him to do. By now, I cared for Les a lot and was growing to love him—perhaps I did love him in the beginning, but I had to sort out my feelings, as this friendship was very different. He was first a very good friend, someone to whom I could talk, and I did talk to him a lot. Then I began to like him; then I grew to love him.

There was a sense of comfort just being with him. I never felt any pressure from him. I always knew what he was thinking and what next to expect from him. He was just a calm and very soothing person who let me have control of my own life. I felt very relaxed in his company. His letters to me came like clockwork, almost one every day. They were filled with great things and planning a wedding in June. I had said to him before he left that if I loved him, I would wait, and if he loved me, then he would come back. I never doubted him, but myself I doubted. What would happen if Deiter did come back? He was never far from my thoughts, but I had to forget him.

5
MORE HEARTACHE

Deiter did come back, and I made the fatal mistake of responding to a telephone call I got at my office. It was Frederick Dempster, who told me that someone wanted to talk to me. It was Deiter at the other end of the telephone line. I thought I would die. Everything seemed to have been in place, for my wedding, and I prided myself on being organized. Now, I was a total wreck. I felt that I had to see him because he needed a face-to-face explanation of what happened to us, although I did feel there hadn't been an "us" for a very long time, and that is why there was a Les. Deiter came over to my house, and we talked a lot, more than we had ever done in all the time we went together. There was no touching, just talking, and that was really difficult because I wanted him to hug me like old times. Then, when he was leaving, he asked if he could have a kiss, so I obliged—and that set me on fire. All I did was kiss him on the cheek. I could not understand myself.

The next day was his mother's birthday, and I had planned to see her and take a present to her. This I had arranged before I knew Deiter was back in the island. I loved his mother; she was a really wonderful lady, and I believe she loved me, too.

I got a ride to her home, and now that I knew that Deiter would be home, I asked him for a ride back to my own home. I ate dinner at his home and talked at length to his mother, as I had always done. Deiter didn't arrive until later, but then we talked for a long while. And then we kissed, and then we cried—at least I cried—and I just knew that I loved this man and could not go through with the wedding. I hurt, my heart ached, and I could not think—I was a total mess. Deiter took me home, but we stopped on the way and we talked forever. I cried forever, we kissed each other forever, and I resolved that I would not marry anyone. I would just run away and be alone forever. I had made a commitment to Les, and I did not want to hurt him, either, but it seemed that I was on a collision path, hurting the people I loved—and I loved two men.

When we arrived at my home, Deiter wanted to come in with me, but I told him that I needed to talk to my parents. I wished I had let him come in with me, though, because all hell broke loose in my house when I told my parents that I was not going to get married. My mother told me that my father had had a heart attack, which I believed. I was not familiar with the symptoms of a heart attack, but I saw him hold his chest and make faces as though he was in pain. But no one called the doctor or took my father to the hospital. The next morning my mother came to my room and re-emphasized what had happened to my father the night before. I got very angry with her, as I was under a great deal of stress, although I did not know it was stress. She slapped me heavily across my face and asked me if I was "man crazy" and called me a "man hurter." I cried and cried and cried. I felt that I could not involve Deiter in all this, and the best thing to do was phone him. I would tell him what had happened and that I was going to marry Les. My parents had spent a lot of money on this wedding. I phoned him with a very heavy heart and told him what had happened.

I went up to Cara's home for the next two days, as her parents sent for me and talked to me to make me feel better. I met Deiter there, and Cara's parents and her brother and sister-in-law talked and talked to us. We never touched or kissed each other again. They advised that we go to see the priests. We did, separately, and I was advised to get married to Les. I also went to the priest that was to marry us, and he told me to get married to Les. He further told me not to tell Les what was happening. I could not do that; I had to tell him. I had to phone Deiter again, and one of the hardest things I have ever had to do in my entire life until then was to tell Deiter Chabot that I could not marry him and that I was going to marry Les.

6

MARRIAGE AND NEW LIFE

I had one week to sort myself out before Les arrived. It was great to see him when he arrived for our wedding. He brought with him the peace that had eluded me for so long, and I felt the calm and serenity that he had brought into my life. He fed to me the serenity that I needed from the maturity he exuded. I felt that I had moved into another realm; I was happy again. I had to tell him that I had seen Deiter and all that had transpired. It was as though he had expected that to happen if I ever saw Deiter again. He appeared to be okay with all that I told him. I told him that I had planned not to get married to anyone and that I had thought about running away. The next week was spent getting things together and getting my immigration papers to enter Canada. I had started the process when I found out that Deiter was going to university in the States. I thought that if I went overseas, I would be on the same continent, and it would be easy to see him, but I didn't understand how great a distance there was.

On June 26, 1965, Les and I got married. It was a beautiful wedding. I opted not to have a dance, as I did not want the festivities to continue into the wee hours of the morning. There were lots of people. Nigel Williams had offered to tape the wedding, but I thought that it would have been too much. Now, I wish I had taken his offer. We had to get to the hotel where we were going to spend a week on our honeymoon. My sister and her boyfriend, who is now her husband, drove us down. We chatted all the way down about all the things that happened at the wedding and how my father just kept standing by me for almost the entire ceremony. I then became quiet on our arrival.

I was still a virgin and had never been alone with a man behind closed doors. Now I was going to be alone with my husband, and I really did not know what to expect. I was extremely nervous. It was a week of intense learning for me as I crossed over the threshold into womanhood. Les confirmed for me the physical side of love.

My office had a surprise going-away party for me. We could not stay to the end, as we did have another commitment. The next few days were a flurry of business, as we had to get shippers in to get wedding presents and my own belongings off to Canada. There were three crates of possessions. Les' father came down for our wedding and was a guest of my family. We left on July 7, 1965, for Canada, with a visa sent by telegram to be used on my entry into Canada. Although I had completed all my medicals and other requirements and was accepted to enter Canada as an immigrant, the visa took some time to get to me. Toronto was my first point of entry, and I had to do another medical there. Everything was fine, and we were off again to catch our flight to Winnipeg, Manitoba.

We had been flying all day from the island to Toronto, and now we were on to Winnipeg. I had never flown in such a large aircraft for such a long time, but I refused to worry about crashing. The plane landed in Nassau, refuelled, and took on more passengers; then we were on our way to Canada. I had flown before at age twelve, but it had been a very small plane. My heart was in my mouth as we flew over the ocean. I then closed my eyes and did not open them again until we landed. I was so scared.

My father-in-law picked up his car from his friends in Winnipeg. His driving made me very nervous, so when we were halfway there and we stopped for a break, I begged Les to drive. It was after three in the morning before we got to our apartment in Brandon, Manitoba.

Our apartment was on the second floor of a three-story house. I was looking for a flat roof, like what I had left at home. I said to myself, *okay, I am going to make the most of this. I have Les. Everything is now new.* Our apartment had one bedroom, a living room, a large kitchen/dining room, and a bathroom with a tub but no shower. Les showed me around and apologized, saying this was all that was available. It was very clean, and I was happy.

We slept until almost three in the afternoon, and then went to get Les' dad, as we had left him to stay with his friends. He came back in with us, now to stay at our place. We went to Les' friends for dinner the following night. They served wild duck and deer, but I just could not eat it; I did, however, try to taste it to be polite, and I almost threw up. Everything was terrible. For the first three days, we ate out, as we were invited to do so. When we finally stayed home, and after Dad had left, Les mentioned that he was hungry. I said that I was hungry also, not remembering that I now had to make the meal—I'd been waiting for the bell to ring to let me know that it was mealtime. Instead, I made some cheese sandwiches. That was our supper.

On the following Saturday, Les' friends and their three children came to spend the day. Donna, Denton's wife, and I went shopping for the odd things I needed for my apartment. When we got back home, I just assumed they would leave, but they stayed. Les told me that I had to make them something to eat. Well, they got cheese sandwiches. What on earth did I know about cooking for people? I did not know anything, but I soon learned to cook. I practiced and practiced. Les became the guinea pig, and he was so good; he never complained—except once, when I made some "rock buns." He sheepishly asked me to throw them out. I learned a lot from the landlady. She taught me how to sew, how to clean the floors, and how to cook Canadian-style.

I spent 1965 through 1967 learning about and getting to know my husband, and he learned about me. We had decided that we would not have any children for two years, as I needed time to get to know and become acclimatized to Canada. I loved horses and learned about several species: Percherons, Belgians, and Clydesdales, which are huge horses with large feet, along with smaller horses that were familiar to me. I attended several rodeos and was impressed with the riding skills of the cowboys as they maneuvered their horses to control their cattle. I spent weekends on the farms of some of my friends and learned how to drive a combine during harvest season. My hair suffered, as it became stiff with the chaff from the wheat.

I wanted to work. My first job was to fill in at a finance company for someone who was on holiday. I discovered by their calculations, on the amounts they loaned to their borrowers, they were getting more from their borrowers than they should. I was to be paid one dollar per hour, as that was what I asked for. I worked for two weeks, but at the end of that time, they did not want to pay me, so Les paid them a visit and brought my pay check home.

I then took a part-time job at an accounting firm as the keypunch operator. I was paid $180 per month. Then I was offered a full-time position at $380 per month, because it was now income tax time. There were several students going for their chartered accountant designations, as the firm was also a school for accountants. I went back to working part-time when income tax time was over. This, to me, was a waste of time, as I wanted full-time employment. My sister was getting married in August 1966, and I was to be her matron of honour. Les told me to quit my job, so that we could both go home to the island. I would find another job when I got back to Canada.

I had always weighed ninety-eight pounds, soaking wet, and could not put weight on. The corner store was nearby, and according to Les, I had a love affair with that store, as I would go there to get a Popsicle or a Creamsicle every night after dinner. These were not the same as the treats I ate on the island; they were delicious. When I saw photos of my sister's wedding, I did not recognize myself—I asked who the girl was. I had put on weight and was up to 110 pounds. I thought I looked healthy.

When we got back to Canada, I was offered a job with the city as a computronic accounting-machine operator, doing the water billing for the city. I loved my job. I also loved the people with whom I worked; they were all so very nice and very funny. I laughed a lot and I love to laugh. I made some very nice friends, some of whom are still my friends today.

7
CHILDREN

Being a military man, Les had a lot of functions to attend, and we entertained a lot. I learned to cook, and everyone liked my meals. I tried and experimented with several recipes as I became more confident with my cooking skills. We moved in 1966 to a two-bedroom apartment that was really nice. We had bought furniture for a two-bedroom apartment that the store kept for us in storage until we moved into a house, closer to Les' job. Well, I could not wait, so I went house-hunting and found this beauty of a place. My husband relented and gave me my way; I loved him. In 1967, we moved into a new apartment that was very private. Everything we had was new. In November, I became pregnant with our first child, my only daughter. I was sicker than a dog, but I survived. The doctor had to make house calls for me, because I was so sick, and couldn't make it to his office. Les hurt his back and landed in the hospital for a couple weeks. That was the first of many hospital stays for him.

My parents were coming up in July 1968. We were now going to put our original plan into action. We moved into a three-bedroom house. It had a huge living room, a huge dining room, and a huge kitchen. The basement had a family room, a laundry room, and a separate furnace room. It was huge, and I learned to clean it. My parents spent three months with us. We had a lot of company. Lucky for me, I could now cook. My mother, who does not like working in the kitchen, helped me a lot.

Our daughter Melani was born on August 13, 1968, in Brandon, Manitoba. The doctor had said she would be born on August 6, and I took that due date literally. I went into the hospital twice and cried when she was not born on the sixth. Les, with his dry humour, stated, "How would the doctor know the date when I was the one who did the deed?" He was very funny and made me laugh a lot.

I must add here that the military life is a very stressful life. I knew this, so I did everything I could to protect my husband from some of the stresses he might encounter; I took care of the stresses of the home. I left my job three months before the baby was born. I tried to follow what I had seen done on the island, as most working mothers to be, left their employment and went on maternity leave about 2 to 3 months before their babies were due. I stayed home for many years while I had my three children. Our first son, Leslie, was born in 1970, also in Brandon, and my second son, Jamie, was born in 1975 in Edmonton.

In 1969, one of my brothers got married, so Les, Melani (who was six months old), and I went to the island for the occasion. It was a very nice wedding. We visited with Cara and her parents and saw Mr. and Mrs. Chabot. I asked them about Deiter and was happy to hear that he was fine. Cara had told me that Deiter got married in 1968 and that he'd had a son in 1969.

When Melani was one year old, we decided it was time to think of a second child, so before I knew what hit me, I was pregnant again, with Leslie. Poor Les—once again he was in the hospital, with a sore back, as he was when I was pregnant with Melani. When Leslie was born, he was jaundiced, and I could not breast-feed him. The worst part of all was that I had to leave him in the hospital when it was time for me to go home. I imagined what it felt like for mothers who carried their babies to term and had a stillbirth. Leslie remained in the hospital for five more days, and I cried for those five days; I had hardly any tears left. I just imagined this helpless little infant lying there and hoped he was being taken care of.

Les was absolutely wonderful as he tried to console and comfort me. Poor little Melani could not understand why Mommy was always crying. She was perplexed. I was the happiest person in the universe when I finally brought my baby home. He was so special. Les, whose unit had been transferred to another province, stayed with me and got permission from his commanding officer to remain with me and then join them later on the "rear party," as it was called. So, after Leslie came home from the hospital, Les left the following week. Now, I was alone with two children—a baby and a toddler of almost two years. Melani, who had been the "perfect child," now began to touch things she had never touched before, especially when I was doing something with Leslie.

Les drove all night, every other weekend, to get home to be with us. It was exciting when he came home, and then sadness crept in when it was time for him to go. He usually arrived on Friday mornings and left again on Sunday mornings. Then he would phone to let me know that he got back safely. He had brought our car back so that I would have some transportation, so he always got a ride down with another person who also was coming to see his wife.

In September of 1970, Les was assigned military housing. He had thought of buying a house, but we decided against it, because there was no guarantee that he would remain at that place for any length of time. That was the military life. After being introduced to military housing, I met a few of the other wives, and I soon learned with whom I wanted to be friends. I always looked for and found my own level, and my friends were really funny—there was lots of laughter at home dinner parties, mess dinners, formal affairs, and dances. Military personnel certainly knew how to enjoy themselves, and they were all so very funny. Some of our very special friends were Vic and Julie, Denton and Donna, who were also the godparents of two of our children, and John and Joan, who were Jamie's godparents. John was a childhood friend of Les'—they had grown up together and had attended the same college together.

In December 1970, we went to the island. My dad had just taken early retirement from his company and moved back to the town where our family had lived. They built another house and were very happy there. In 1971, our family went to the island again for Christmas and New Year's. It was nice to see all the children together, enjoying each other. I got carried away as I tried to enjoy eating my favourite dishes and soon found out that I could no longer eat my most favourite island dishes. After eating "ackee and salt fish," I was deathly ill with stomach cramps, cold sweats, and fainting. My aunt, who is a nurse, saw to it that I got over my illness. My husband had a worried look on his face, and many years later, he told me a secret he had carried for years. He was so very scared every time that I became sick, but he never showed any weakness, because he always had to be the strong one, or so he thought. I was worried whenever he was sick, but apart from his back problems, that was very rare.

In 1972, Les was chosen to go on a six-month safety course, which had now become another part of his job. He had been an airborne engineer. His job had always been an "elite" job, with a specialist's pay and a risk allowance, which meant he had to make many parachute jumps per month, using any parachute packed by others. He was a test parachute jumper.

The parachutes that were used by any member of the forces whose career called for jumping came from Les' unit; therefore, all the members of the unit were required to jump also.

My husband never brought his job home. Home was for family, and I liked it that way. However, if I knew there was a problem, I would try to alleviate some of the stress he might be experiencing in whatever way I could. It was always a very stressful situation when someone got hurt on a parachute jump, although this did not happen very often.

He decided that when he left on this six-month safety course, the children and I should spend the time with my parents on the island. They were overjoyed. Most of my friends were in the capital, but being in the country, I did not see them very often. When Les' course was over, he flew back home, got rid of his military gear, and four hours later, he was on an eight-hour flight to the island. I knew he was coming, but I did not know when.

We wrote each other almost every day. I was pleasantly surprised when my father woke me up from an afternoon nap with my children to ask me to come to the veranda, and there I saw my husband walking in to my parents' house with his suitcase. He looked so fit from all that exercise. This, however, was not my plan. I was waiting on a letter from him to tell me which day he would arrive, as my parents were going to keep the children while he and I went off to a resort for some rest and relaxation. That never did materialize, even though I had all this money to make the reservations.

Les had suggested that I open a bank account on the island, as he could then assign me a pay allotment so that the children and I would not need for anything or depend on my parents for anything. He came for three weeks, and then we were all on our way back to Canada, as he had come to take us all home. This was now July 1972. He learned that his posting was to become permanent, so we decided to buy our own home. In November 1972, we bought and built our first house and watched it go up. It was really exciting, as we chose what we wanted—building, exterior and interior, carpets, flooring, fixtures ... everything. In March 1973, we moved in, and I loved it.

I was very active during the years that I was at home with my children. I learned to sew some of my own clothes—not that I had to, but I wanted to. I put in a vegetable garden every year and pickled and preserved what I could. I made jams and jellies, and I baked bread. I was in a learning spurt, and I enjoyed doing all these things. And let's not forget my flowers. My favourite plants are wild roses of all colors. I would go to the nursery, and buy my potted plants every year, and plant them wherever I saw fit—in flower boxes and around my trees. I went back to work in the accounting field as soon as the children started school.

I began to get sick, and did not know why. My heart would race, and I was losing weight and would cry for no reason at all. I thought I was going to die, as my muscles would contract, and I shook at intervals for no reason whatsoever. Les was worried. I was further distressed when the doctor told me that I had an overactive thyroid condition. Now, I was really upset; I was now defective. I had never had anything wrong with me—that bothered me on top of everything else. That year, Les' dad, who had been a widower for many years, decided to remarry, and he and his new wife went to Jamaica for six months. They came back in March 1974. She went on to Saskatchewan to fix up their new home, while Les' dad stopped in Winnipeg to get his medical check-up—he was a veteran of two world wars who had been gassed, and he had also had an ulcer operation in which a part of his stomach was removed. I could no longer work, as I was now sick.

I was admitted to the hospital to have my thyroid operation. I had spoken to my mother-in-law on the Friday and went into the hospital on the Sunday. She had a stroke on Sunday night. Dad flew from Winnipeg to his home in Saskatchewan on Monday, phoned Les, and asked him to come down from Edmonton to Saskatchewan. Les could not, as I was in the hospital, and he had taken time off from work to care for the children. So he told Dad to phone his other son Carl, one of Les' brothers, who was two years younger than Les. Well, Mom died the next day, Monday. My operation was scheduled for Thursday. Les came in every evening to see me, but he did not tell me about Mom. He was at the hospital for my surgery in the morning, and he was there after my surgery, which was a long one, and then he was off to see his Dad—about four hours away by car. By the time he got there, all four sons were there. The funeral was on Friday. In the interim, Dad had a heart attack, so he ended up in the hospital and was unable to attend his wife's funeral.

Les came back home and came to the hospital on Saturday morning. He then told me everything that had happened. This set me back a bit. I was due to get out of the hospital on the following day, on Sunday, but Les felt that I should stay. I did not want to, so the doctor released me, and Les came to take me home. It was really nice to be back home and in my own bed. It was good to see my children, and I just wanted to love my husband, as I saw the stress and worry in his face.

The following morning, Les took Melani to kindergarten and went back to pick her up at 11.00. He had just entered the house when the telephone rang, and it was his oldest brother, calling to tell him that Dad had just passed away. Les told him what to do, as he was the executor of his father's will. Then, he collapsed on the kitchen chair and just cried. He had had enough. I could only hug him because I was also at a loss for words. Within five days, they were both gone. His brother Carl had just gotten home to Calgary when he got the message, so he just turned around, drove up to our house, picked up Les and their younger brother Ted, and drove all night to get back to Saskatchewan, where their father lived.

Ted's wife stayed with me and the children. Then, the following day, Les' best friend and the children's godfather, Denton, came to pick us up and took us to his home, where we stayed until Les came back home on Friday. Denton's wife, Donna, had also been in the hospital and came home about the same time as I did, so Denton had to babysit us all. He cooked all the meals and also took care of the children. That was a terrible time. Recovery from my operation took some time, and Les thought we should move back into Edmonton from the suburbs where we lived, about twenty-eight miles out. I went into hysterics at the suggestion. I had put a lot of myself into our house, and I did not want to move. When I became more rational, I saw his point. He worked in Edmonton, and if we were sick, it would take him some time to drive back in case of emergency—there had been so much sickness and death lately. I also had a fear of going into my basement because Les had brought home some of his father's artifacts, and his Wellington boots were visible, minus the person who wore them., I was saddened at the sight, because he was no longer with us to wear them.. The Salvation Army could not come fast enough to take these donations, as the boots were included.

We sold our house at more than double the price we had paid for it. We bought another house in Edmonton. Melani started first grade at the Catholic school nearby. I had the most wonderful neighbours. They were farmers, who had to sell their farm because of the health of their only daughter. She had brittle bones that broke very easily. She had to have many operations to put steel into her bones so they would not break. Today, although her body shows the challenges of her growing years, she is married, and she is a beautiful, independent person—a very short body, very long arms, and very long legs. She works and drives, and I don't think there is anything she cannot do, except, of course, have children.

While packing to move to Edmonton, I could not understand why

I was not feeling well. I had a few spells where I felt faint, but I sort of over looked it, as I was still on the mend from my operation. My doctor told me that it would take at least ten years for my metabolic rate to get back to normal. I went to the doctor once we moved and was told that I was pregnant with my third child. I became concerned for the welfare of the baby and hoped all would be well for this child. My husband was concerned about my health, but all was well. My second child was five years old.

8

PARACHUTE ACCIDENT

In August 1974, Les was to make three parachute jumps on one particular day. The first two went well, but he was not so fortunate on his third descent. I was at home when the telephone rang; it was his commanding officer, who told me that Les had been hurt. He was taken by ambulance to the hospital and would be later transferred to the military hospital. He had several broken bones and a dislocated shoulder, and because of his thick, muscular build, they had a lot of difficulty trying to get his arm back into the shoulder socket. They had to stand on him to get it back in place, so apart from the pain he was experiencing from his injuries, his body was also badly bruised. By the time I reached the hospital, he was heavily sedated. His arm was taped to his body, and he could not move it. I brought his car home, and on the passenger seat was his lunchbox with his uneaten lunch that I had made for him that morning. My stomach was now in knots as I soon realized that he could have been killed. This fear engulfed me, as I thought of what could have been. I was thankful to God that he was alive. I was four months pregnant. He was released from the hospital a week later but was off work for six months, with his left arm taped to his side—and Les was left-handed. He had several months of physical therapy, and he was assigned a military driver to take him to and from the hospital for his treatments.

Our son Jamie was born February 24, 1975. Les took me to the hospital at 3:00 AM, and on the way, he ran just about every red light. I was in agony, and the doctor induced labour at about 6:30 AM. He then went to do an operation, planning to return to deliver the baby, but at

8:00, an intern delivered Jamie. Les had been in the delivery room for each of our children and had specific jobs cut out for him. The first was support for me, and the other was to cut the umbilical cord of the baby. This time, he was shown to the wrong room, and by the time he located me, I had already had the baby. He was very angry and made it known to the maternity room staff.

In June 1975, Les was told that he was being transferred to a base in Saskatchewan. He could no longer jump or test parachutes, so he was now categorized for light duties. He was responsible for a crew of men and all the safety on the military aircrafts that trained pilots, including their world-renowned military aerobatic team. His extra-curricular activity was as a hockey coach for his unit team. They were good; they won the base championship and the Western Finals.

We put our house in Edmonton up for sale and went on a house-hunting trip to our new place of posting, at the expense of the military. The builders were on strike, so we could not have a home built—that had been our intention—so we bought a home that was eight months old. We were there in time for Melani to start grade two and for Leslie to start kindergarten. Jamie was six months old.

This was our second military move. We lived in a hotel for one month until our house was ready. This house was not very far from the children's school, but it was also on a corner, which turned out to be very busy and dangerous, due to the number of accidents that took place there. I was concerned about our children's safety. This house had many added features but not enough to keep me there, so I went looking for vacant land to purchase, in order to build a house. I was successful, and again, we built a beautiful home with many added features. We moved there in December 1976. It was a lot of land, so we had a very big vegetable garden and a big lawn, lots of flowers, and a beautiful hedge that made our home very private. I loved my house.

In 1977, my cousin was assassinated on the island. He was high up in the government there. That summer, we all went to Toronto to grieve with other members of our family. In 1978, Les was told that he was being transferred to Germany. I cried, because I did not want to go. I had started to work again, in finance on the military base, and I really liked my job. I had only been working there for eleven months. This also meant that the children would be disrupted as they were in several activities, hockey, and dancing, and T-ball, and soccer, and baseball. Now, they were also being uprooted from their friends. But then, that had been the story of our lives.

We were only in our house a little over a year, and I had put so much into this house. We also, had made a lot of friends—for the first time, there were people from the Caribbean, Guyanese, Canadians, Filipinos, and other nationalities. We met them all and had several dinner parties and were invited to many.

We sold our house, our cars, and our appliances—sold, sold, sold—as we could not store some of these things. The military stored the rest of our furniture and effects for the four years we were going to be away. We took with us the bare essentials, as the military provided a furnished apartment for us with everything new. I think it was the time limit of four years that got to me. I had dealt with that time frame before when a university and a town left a very bitter taste in my mouth. However, this time was different. I resigned myself to the fact that I had to be in Germany for four years, as this was Les' job. In July 1978, we were on our way to Lahr in the Federal Republic of Germany. Our flight on the military aircraft to Germany was seven hours long. We had flown Air Canada from Regina to Winnipeg, then by military aircraft from Winnipeg to Trenton, Ontario, where we changed planes to another military aircraft and flew to Ottawa, the capital. This was my first experience flying in a military passenger jet. It was crowded.

9
MOVE TO GERMANY

We arrived in Germany, dead tired. It was raining, it was damp, and everything was green—the grass was green, the trees were green, and all the military buildings were green. Each new military personnel that arrived was assigned a sponsor from the unit, to whom he would report. Our sponsors were very nice. Our house was not quite ready, so they housed us in temporary quarters on the main military base. This eventually became our permanent quarters for the next three years. On our first weekend in Germany, we experienced an earthquake that generated a lot of damage. This was the last thing I expected, and my nerves were on edge.

I had never been exposed to total military life, as we had lived in our own homes off the base, except for twice when we moved for short periods of time. Now, I had to be here for four years, living among personnel from all across Canada and from all walks of life. Again, the four-year time limit resounded in my head—I had not done too well with that sentence before. I was very apprehensive and had talked myself out of being depressed, but now, I was not going to be alone and uncertain anymore—I had Les and the children. I learned really fast that not all Canadians are the same. The western Canadians, which we were, were quite different from the eastern Canadians, or the Maritimers, or the Newfoundlanders. Our children, who loved the outdoors, did not want to go out, because they felt intimidated by the older kids who were there before we arrived, therefore they had to learn to protect themselves. It took them a while to venture out; therefore, they have their own tales of Germany

Les decided that he was going to buy a European car, and then decided against it, so he ordered a new American car, a Ford Zephyr station wagon, from the factory in Belgium. It took a few weeks to be delivered. I felt that I had stepped backward in time. Our apartment was on the top floor of a three-story building, and there were no elevators. It was six flights of stairs up, and seven down to the laundry. I did a lot of crying. It was a chore to bring groceries in. Finally, we got settled in, and I learned to appreciate the different lifestyle and tried to learn the language. Television was my window to the German lifestyle. It helped a lot, and the words I learned are with me today. The children did pick up a bit of the language. Jamie, who was three years old, watched *Sesame Street* in German every day. Leslie was eight, and Melani was ten years old.

Some of the best Canadian teachers were recruited to educate our children, and they excelled. Accolades were given and awards were presented to Melani and Leslie at the end of each school year. Jamie started junior kindergarten there. We enjoyed eating German food and visited their *gasthauses* (inns) quite often for schnitzel and *pomme frites* (French fries). Then there was the bratwurst and Brochins, which were the most delicious, fresh crusty buns that were baked daily. I am not a beer drinker, but beer was everywhere. It was a diet staple for Germans—and, I must add, some Canadians. I liked German wine at meals, especially when we entertained friends. My limit was one glass, and I didn't always fill it to the top of the goblet. In Canada, our children were accustomed to wine at our Sunday meals. One very small liqueur glass of wine was their limit—a very small taste.

The military had their own shopping center, and one of the first things that we did was to buy a freezer and fill it with a side of beef, a side of pork, some chickens, and other staples that we constantly shared with our friends. We also went shopping on the American bases' shopping centers, specifically Kaiserslautern, to stock up on dry and canned staples, as their goods were less expensive. We paid in American dollars, and it was a better rate of exchange on the American bases. We exchanged students—we had American children at our home, and my children went to their homes. Our children were also exposed to a lot of French, not only in school but from friends we made. One of our dearest friends was a couple from the French armed forces. He was the French liaison officer between the French and Canadian forces. We exchanged visits of our children—ours to be saturated with French, and theirs to be saturated with English. The boys were also enrolled in hockey. Leslie was a really good hockey player, so we sent him to a hockey school in Switzerland for two weeks. Of course, being a mother, I worried about him; he was only ten years old. I could hardly wait to go with Les to pick him up. I just loved to watch him play junior and midget hockey; he was good. Today, he is still a very good hockey player, and he still plays hockey for recreation when he can.

My husband, as was all other military personnel, was always on call for duty, and ever so often, there were exercises in which the men were gone for a couple days. The sirens would go off, indicating an attack. They would scramble into safety suits and be out of their houses in a flash. We called this safety suit a "poopy suit"—after being in it for a couple days, it was not very hygienic. I decided to wash one of Les' suits, but I did not know that it was filled with a charcoal filter. Obviously, the washing machine became black from the charcoal, and I had to do a special wash to get the machine clean. I'd put the suit in the dryer and had to clean that, too. I never washed another one. Les just got another one reissued.

Our first trip was to Garmisch-Partenkirchen. We spent a week at an old and beautiful German Officers Mess that was converted into a hotel and now belonged to the American military. The accommodations were very good. From there we took a day trip with other American military personnel and their families to Innsbruck, Austria. There we visited the Olympic site. We took the Bavaria Zugspitze Railway to the summit of the Zugspitze, the highest point in the Alps. It is the best panoramic view in Europe, as one can see the Bavarian, Austrian, Italian, and Swiss Alps, among other beautiful scenery. As I am not a lover of heights, so I found this height a little scary and did not want to venture too close to the rails to look at the people skiing down below—that area was conducive to great skiing. We stayed for another week and visited several other points of interest. I found that Garmisch-Partenkirchen was very similar to our national parks in Alberta, Canada, specifically Banff National Park. It was beautiful there, but we had to go home, back to Baden Soellingen, where we lived.

A few months later, my brother, his wife, and their three children came to visit us. We had planned to take them on a trip to Italy, so we got someone to come in to our home to take care of the children while we were away. We went to Oberammergau, Austria, where the Passion of Christ is performed every ten years, and we visited several areas; then we were on our way to Dobbiaco, Italy. We went across the Dolomite Mountains to Cortina d'Ampezzo, another Olympic site, where Nancy Green, a Canadian skier, won the gold medal for Canada. We stayed on the mainland of Italy, had lunch, and then went by water taxi to Venice, where we toured San Marcos Island. We visited the church where St. Paul the Apostle is buried, as well as St. Mark's Square, where all the pigeons congregated and where a member of our tour group almost lost her purse. We toured St. Mark's Basilica and a glass-blowing factory that produced some absolutely beautiful glass works. I bought a replica of a gondola, which I still have today.

We went back by a motor launch to the mainland, as the water taxi operators went on strike. We had dinner at the hotel and that night, we went back to San Marcos Island, Venice, to sail on the gondolas. Several gondoliers were hired to take our group in the wide open waters. The gondolas made a formation, and the gondoliers serenaded us all. That was really a treat. The next day, we went to San Marino, where Les got hit in the crosswalk by a girl riding a small motorcycle. After much ado, we then went on to Rome. I loved Rome. We toured the city, went to the Colosseum, then to the Vatican and St. Peter's Basilica. I was totally impressed. We went to the catacombs, where the Christians were buried— that was very depressing. We went to the Palazzo Venezia, the Capitol, and many churches, the remains of the Roman Forum, the aqueducts, St. Paul's Basilica, the parliament buildings, the ancient Appian Way, Trevi Fountain, and the Pantheon, among other sights of interest. I believe I saw everything there was to see, and I liked what I saw. We had a night out in Rome, so we went to the Spanish Steps, and I bartered in the Piazza; then I had as many flavours of gelato as I could possibly get on one cone and ate them all.

The following day, we went to be blessed by Pope John Paul II, or as the Germans say, "Johannes Paulus de Switzen," or as Italians say, the "Papa." He was not at the Vatican, so we went to his summer home at Castel Gandolfo. To climb that hill for his blessing was penance enough. We were not disappointed, as he came out on his balcony and blessed us all in several languages. His summer garden was beautiful and was absolutely crowded with other souls who came for his blessings. This was the highlight of my Italian trip.

From there, we traveled to Sorrento. We stayed at Castellammare and went into Sorrento the following day for our trip to the Isle of Capri. We spent all day in and out of boats in the middle of the Mediterranean. We sailed by the ruins of Emperor Caesar Augustus' summer home and the homes of movie stars to get to the Blue Grotto. We ventured in the Blue Grotto in the middle of the ocean, transferring from a big launch into a canoe. I had to lie on my back to enter this cave. Inside, it was blue and beautiful and very, very deep. I could not believe I had done that. Later, I really scared myself half to death, just thinking of what could have happened if the canoe had capsized. I would probably have drowned; as I cannot swim we spent all day in Capri. There are no cars on the island and to get to the top of the island from the boat docks, a cable car was the mode of transportation. The scenery was beautiful from the summit. We toured around and looked at all the Roman artefacts, and we had lunch, which consisted of fish that was really good—and lots of it. We sailed back to the mainland, got back to the hotel, had dinner, and then a party was put on for us that night.

The next day, we toured Pompeii. I was very impressed. I love archaeology and anthropology and have often said that I would have liked to have studied that in university instead. I was absolutely fascinated with the ingenuity of the inhabitants of so very long ago—and to think that some of these discoveries are being used today, such as running water through metal pipes. The wheels of the chariots from constant movement as they drove through the narrow streets were grooved into the streets. A stepping stone was placed in the middle of the streets for the inhabitants to get from one side of the street to the other. The width of the grooves made by the chariot wheels in the streets were used in the measurements for our vehicles today.

We then went to Naples for lunch, then on to Florence for two days. We visited the gold and silver market and bought jewellery and a good Italian leather handbag. We toured the churches and saw a copy of Michelangelo's statue of David—the original is in the Academy Gallery. I loved that statue, and I now have a small replica that is displayed in my home. We then drove back to Germany through Switzerland. We picked up our car, and then drove to Baden. At first, I had not wanted to go on this trip to Italy and was trying to talk Les into going with just my brother and his wife, and I would stay with the children. That suggestion did not go over too well, as Les flatly refused, stating that if I did not go, neither would he. So I had to go—and I really enjoyed myself.

10

TRIP TO GREECE

The year 1979 rolled by quickly, as we were so busy with entertaining and with the kids going on trips and going to hockey and baseball—all three had their own curriculums. Les and I got in a few day trips. We had company from England and Spain, who were our guests for three weeks.

During that period, I was wearing a cast on my right wrist due to overuse syndrome, as I was told. I was frustrated without the proper use of my hand. I am right-handed and really felt like smashing the cast against the wall to get rid of it. It did not make sleeping very easy, either, and Les suffered several blows as I turned over in my sleep. In 1980, after being at home again for two years, being the proverbial housewife, taking children to and picking them up from school, Les got a call at work—our home had no telephone—requesting my attendance at an interview for a job at the Military Community Center. I was not sure that I wanted to attend, as we were leaving on a trip to Greece the day after the scheduled interview, and I had lots of planning to do. However, my better judgment prevailed, and it told me not to turn down the interview when they were interested in me. My referral had come from Canada to Lahr and on to Baden. I decided I had to go to that interview, which I did, and then I would forget about getting that job.

We went off on our trip to Greece. Our route took us through Switzerland and Italy by boat, for two days and two nights, sailing across the Mediterranean. Our bunks on the ship rolled from side to side as the ship glided through the water. I felt as if I was sleeping in a baby's sleeping cot. It was not too bad. Les did not like sleeping in the top bunk, so he bunked with me, and we rocked together. There was lots of entertainment and good food across the Mediterranean, with a stop at Corfu. We passed Albania to our first port of entry at Patras, Greece. I will never forget my first sight as we came on deck. Everything was painted white with some blue, and the haunting song of "Welcome to Greece" was being played on the ship's loud speakers. Oh! My heart just filled with so much emotion! I will always remember Greece.

We then boarded a tour bus, and our first stop on land was Olympia, the starting place of the Olympic Games. It was just a bunch of ruins, but the area where the lighting of the Olympic torch and the ceremony was held was cordoned off but very visible. We went into the ancient stadium, which now is a large area with grass, trees, and shrubbery, and to my surprise, the original starting line of all ancient Olympic events was still there. This line is worn, but it is made of marble, and it is very visible. My impression and my imagination gathered momentum, as I am a great fan of history, especially Greek and Roman history, and I imagined Alexander the Great performing in this arena. I once saw the movie in which Alexander the Great was portrayed by Richard Burton, the movie actor, so for me, I associated Burton with Alexander the Great, and he was so handsome.

Our first meal in Greece was at a very small and quaint restaurant in Olympia. We feasted on lamb shish kebabs, salad, and hard Greek bread. Now, I was never a lover of lamb, and neither was my husband, but we looked at each other and began to eat. I did not like the idea of eating it a little rare, but I was hungry, so I ate it. Now, we were game for anything, and later, we learned that we were about to eat lamb in every form possible.

From Olympia, we drove across the Greek countryside to Corinth, where we stopped for the night. Again, I was impressed, because I was now in a place I had only read about in the Bible and where ancient saints had trod. We went for dinner, then to the disco, with Greek music and dancers. I did think it odd to see young teenage boys—some were our waiters—dancing with and jumping on each other, making hissing sounds. My husband had been drinking ouzo, a very potent Greek drink that tastes and smells like licorice. He knew about this drink, having spent a year and a half in Egypt, the Golan Heights, on a United Nations Peacekeeping tour. He did not drink that much, but when he got up to go to ask the band to play other music, instead of walking toward the band, his legs took him away, so we kept walking to our hotel room. There was nothing wrong with his head; it was clear and his language was coherent, but his legs were like rubber and had a mind of their own. I did laugh at him, as he did have a love affair with the toilet bowl, as his stomach felt unsettled, and so he held on to it for security. We were up early and he stated that his head and his hearing was so sharp he could hear the "poppies grow," while we were at a rest stop as our bus stopped for us to stretch our legs. He picked me a flower presented it to me, and I have the picture to prove it. My husband has always been a very sharp man, mentally, and today, he was a lot sharper. I laughed at him all day and without sympathy. I so loved him.

We drove across country again, and went to a Greek amphitheatre at Epidaurus. There, we sat on the stone seats where people many years ago sat to enjoy the theater. The seats were very comfortable. We then listened to a demonstration of the acoustics by someone's dropping a coin on the ground in the middle of the performing area. It was clearly heard. I was impressed that people of so long ago just simply knew what they were doing, and some of that ingenuity is being used today. From there, we then went to Nauplia, where we had lunch. I had Greek moussaka for the first time. I later learned to make this dish and have served it many times at my own dinner parties. Across from the mainland, was a prison on an island that was not accessible to us. We then went up to King Agamemnon's tomb and the ruins of his palace in Mycenae. It was situated on top of a mountain, and it was a bit of a climb to get through the Gate of Lions, but we made it. The ruins of his castle are still visible, and the tiles that adorned his floors are still there, after so many years. His tomb is built just with rocks—no cement to hold anything together; there is just one huge rock in the middle of the overhead that spans the entrance that keeps everything intact. It was a huge tomb and dark inside, and I did not venture too far inside, for fear of encountering the spirit of the king that I was not prepared to meet.

On our way to Delphi, we went across the Peloponnesus, across the Isthmus of Corinth, which is a man-made isthmus that was cut in 1893 and was built to make the distance between Piraeus and the Adriatic Sea 325 kilometres shorter. This channel is six kilometres long and eight meters in depth and is very impressive. In Delphi we wandered through yet another set of ruins. We went through some more countryside, and I began to read the signs and knew where we were going, as the tour guide had given me a copy of the Greek alphabet—I still have that piece of paper to this day. I was very proud of myself for learning the alphabet so quickly—it was as if a veil had been lifted, and then I could see.

We went by ferry to get across to another area on the mainland so that we could drive to Athens—another long drive. We were to spend the next three days and nights in Athens. Well, I was almost run over by a truck disembarking from the ferry. Les pulled me out of the way in the nick of time, or I would have been killed (and I am not about to compare drivers from any part of the world). We got on our bus and headed for Athens. I loved Athens, a city that never sleeps. After dinner, we went to the Plaka, the area for Greek nightlife and entertainment. There were bands, music, food, and a lot of dancing. We walked back to our hotel at 3:00 AM, past street vendors selling food and other wares, all dressed in suits. We also saw ladies of the night behind glass doors, calling at men to come hither. I firmly held on to my husband.

The following day we took a trip to the island of Aegina. It was uneventful, except for the bus ride across the island, during which I thought for sure the local driver was about to kill us all. (News flash: "Canadians killed in bus crash on Greek Island.") The bus appeared to be wider than the road itself. The following day we toured Athens. We went to the Panathenaic Stadium, where the recent Olympic Games were held; saw the presidential palace and the guards dressed in the beautiful uniforms (they looked really handsome); saw the seats of parliament; and went to the Acropolis and saw the Parthenon. The view and the scenery from there was just amazing. Athens lay out in front of us. The Acropolis just looked like a mass of stones and broken columns, some upright and some down. The remains of the temples of Athena and Zeus stood upright and were very impressive. At the foot of the Acropolis was a small amphitheatre, called an odeum, where there was a performance of light. We saw the Constitution Square and the Omonia Square. We saw the university, the Academy of Athens, and the Zappeion. I really enjoyed all this.

We had lamb stew for dinner. We had a free night, so Les and I just walked around. It seemed that wherever Les and I went in our travels, someone would end up with us, so another couple joined us on our walkabout. We had the following day free again, so we decided to go shopping. We went into a clothing store because I saw a skirt that was of interest to me. It was made with a heavy cotton material that I assumed was made in Greece. I only wanted to look at it, but we could not get out of the store, as the saleslady was determined that we should buy something. Because I knew that we could barter, I came up with the lowest and most ridiculous price ever in drachmas. She could not let me have it for that price, so I began to walk out, as by now Les had left me on my own—he does not like to barter and felt embarrassed.

I did get the skirt, although I really did not want it, but it is a Greek tradition that the first customer who enters a store should not leave without buying something, as this will bring good luck to the shopkeeper for the day; there will be bad luck if nothing is bought. So I said to Les that we were not very smart—we should have gone into a jewellery store first! We visited one later and got some jewellery—a pair of Greek earrings for me, chains for the boys, and a charm bracelet for Melani. The owner of the jewellery store brought out some beautiful pieces of jewellery to show us that were all handmade. He wanted Les and me to take it back to Germany with us, where we could choose what we wanted at our leisure, and then send the rest back to him. I said, "You have got to be kidding?" He was dead serious. We declined his offer fiercely, as I had no intention of going to jail or visiting my husband while he was in military confinement, waiting to be shipped back to Canada, perhaps to real civilian jail. The jeweller did not even know us, but he said he knew an honest face when he saw one, and we both had honest faces. That was a nice compliment, but we were not too sure about him and wondered what sort of a setup this was. Obviously, we went our merry way without his jewellery. We have laughed about this so many times.

The following day we drove across country again on our way back to Patras, as we had to sail back to Italy. This took another two days and two nights to get back to Italy, and there was a lot of dancing and other forms of entertainment on the ferry. I discovered the slot machines and having never played them before; I decided to do so to use up the drachmas we had left. I lost them all and could not get another red cent from my husband. On our trip back to Italy, we had the opposite cabin structure. The beds in our cabin were now horizontal, they laid across the ship from east to west and we now rocked from head to toe; consequently, all night our heads and our toes felt as though they were being filled with more blood than necessary. I felt that one part or the other of my anatomy was about to explode, and that was very uncomfortable. I felt like a bottle of hot sauce that was being shaken before use.

We got to Italy in the late afternoon, and we had a long ride back to Germany. We did not stop until we got to Switzerland, where we had a late dinner and then were on our way again to Lahr, Germany. We picked up our car and drove the sixty-eight kilometres to Baden. We got home about 3:00 AM; we were really, really tired. Our children were with our neighbour, and they came bounding in quite early, wanting to know what we brought back for them. A silver chain each for Leslie and Jamie, a bracelet full of charms for Melani, a soccer ball each for Leslie and Jamie, and a big, thick Greek sweater for Melani.

After we hugged our children, Les went off to work, the children went to school, and I had some more rest. I checked the mail and could hardly contain myself or wait to tell Les of the news I received—my job offer at an exorbitant salary, the highest of any civilian job on the base. It also meant that Les could drop me off at work on his way to his place of employment in the morning and pick me up every evening on his way home. This was going to be just fine.

11

TRIP TO LOURDES, PARIS, HOLLAND, AND SPAIN

I loved my job. I kept about fifty-two accounts of the various community services and amenities for the base, which included a tour bus operation. I bought all the foreign currency for all the countries our bus passed through. I loved this; it was fun. I worked with Deutsche marks and converted them into every other currency. I loved working with figures, and better yet, my job allowed me to travel on the bus for free, anywhere. I had to pay for my hotel accommodations and my meals, and my husband, who was in the military, had to pay to travel on the bus, plus his hotel and meals. We took a lot of day tours together. We went to Strasbourg, the seat of the French parliament, and we went to the Black Forest, where they made the cuckoo clocks. We went to Baden-Baden to see the famous casinos and the Roman bath houses, among other places.

Our church had asked for volunteers to go on a military pilgrimage to Lourdes. I asked Les if he was interested, but he said he would not volunteer for anything, nor would he hold up his hands in church for fear they might think he was volunteering for something. So, unbeknown to him, I put his name on the volunteer list. When we got back from Greece, the padre called Les and told him that he was one of the people chosen to go. Les was not upset with me for putting his name on the list; he just accepted the fact that he was going, and that he had to be in his uniform for the entire weekend, and that he had a lot of marching and standing to do. I could not contain my laughter at his misery. I could not go, as it was for the men only, so I stayed home with the children. Sometimes, if not most of the time, wives know what is best for their husbands. As it turned out, Les was so happy that he went, as it was an opportunity of a lifetime. There were military personnel there from all over the world. He said it was very moving, and he was glad that he'd had the opportunity to go. I still have the holy water in the Virgin Mary plastic container they all got and filled to take home. I also have some good photos of his experience. I played a lot of tricks on my husband; he was so much fun.

Les and I went to Paris. I liked it, but since he had been there before and I had not, he only went because I wanted to go. We saw the sights, and he climbed the stairs at the Sacré-Coeur, the Basilica of the Sacred Heart of Jesus. It is a Roman Catholic Church, and a very popular landmark. We went down Champs-Elysees, a very prestigious avenue in Paris, perhaps one of the most famous avenues in the world for shopping, then to the Arc de Triomphe, one of the greatest and most historical arches in the world. It was built to commemorate victories of battles fought by French Troops. We then went to the Eiffel Tower to the second level, as the third level was being renovated. This is a world famous tower that was built for the World Exhibition. The top of the tower can be seen from all over Paris. Then we went to the Louvre, one of the largest museums in the world that displays the most famous works of art, the Mona Lisa, the Venus de Milo and many more beautiful pieces of art. Our hotel was in the area of the opera, and that room was painted black with a very hard roll on the bed for a pillow, which Les pounded into submission every night to try to soften it up. I just could not contain myself and just cracked up like an idiot, while he beat the pillow. I can't say I liked the food.

Les waited all weekend for Monday to take me to get a *donair* which is a Mediterranean style pita bread sandwich made with beef or lamb, and served with a sauce that resembles honey mustard because I had never eaten one before, and Les liked them, as he had eaten them in the Middle East. He told the vendor that he liked donairs, so the vendor took some meat that had fallen in the lamb tallow and made a donair for Les and one for me .Well, Les took one taste of it, and because he didn't really like lamb, he could not eat it; he threw it in the garbage. Here again, I just could not stop laughing at the faces he made and the disappointment that he showed. I tried to eat mine; I thought it was all right, as I did not know what to expect, but with my giggling, Les convinced me that I did not like mine either and that I should throw it away. I was laughing so hard at his disappointment that I had to sit on the sidewalk, holding my donair and telling him how good I thought it was. Well, I did get rid of it, as it was terrible. I laughed a lot.

We had done the *Bateau Mouche* which is a sightseeing boat, the night before. This boat sailed up and down the Seine River as we were served a sumptuous meal of many courses. Lobster was the first course, so my stomach was not feeling that well. All I really wanted was some soup. There was none, so I ended up having some stew which I thought might have been horsemeat, as it was very spongy and as I had never eaten any meat so spongy in my whole life. After that one taste, it was out of my mouth in a flash, and I did not eat any more. Later that night, we went to the Follies Bergère. This was okay and entertaining—a lot of naked people and lots of flesh. The following day, we were on our way back to Germany.

My husband got hurt again on his job and spent some time in the hospitals in Lahr and Kaiserslautern, as well as bed rest at home, flat on his back for a while. When he did go back to work, he had to be put on light duty again. He probably should have never been sent to Germany because of all the problems he had with a bad back and a dislocated shoulder. After Christmas and New Year's of 1981, when Les was well enough, we took the children with us to Holland. We went to the Keukenhof Gardens, where the Tulip Festival was held and where there is every variety of tulips one can think of—this was absolutely beautiful. They adorned our bus with a garland of tulips. We visited two war memorials, and the one at Arnhem and Nijmegen brought heavy tears to my eyes when I read the ages of the soldiers that were killed in the Second World War—all Canadians. We wrote our names in the guest book in 1981. Our children had an enjoyable time in Holland; they each came home with a pair of wooden shoes, among other things.

We walked down "canal" street, where the call girls were paraded in showcases. The children wanted to know what the girls were doing. I don't know what their father told them, but in the meantime, my jaw dropped as I stared and consequently, I walked into an iron pylon, almost killing myself. We visited Rotterdam, Volendam, and Madurodam—a miniature city geared for children. Jamie was in his element, and we had difficulty getting him to leave. We took a boat tour on the Amstel River, which proved very interesting. Many people live on the river in houseboats. I enjoyed our visit to Holland. While there, I recalled what I had said about Leonard Darrow, from boarding school days—he was always crying for something. Well, Jamie became Leonard, as he demonstrated this trait at Madurodam.

On our way back to Germany, we went through Rheims, and I remembered my history, which involved Martin Luther and the Catholic

Church. It was here also that I encountered one washroom for both men and women. The urinals for the men were visible with their patrons when the women had to go in to use their own toilets. I did not like this, so I did not go in. It was here, too, that we ordered steaks that were cooked on one side only. Les sent them back three times to have them cooked properly. In the end, we could not eat them because they were burned.

Les was transferred back to Canada, and Saskatchewan, where we lived before, was to be his place of residence. I did not like that, as we had sold our house there. We were due to leave Germany in July 1981. There were a few things we still had to do. The children's school year ended in May. They got their awards, and we left shortly after for a trip to Spain, to a place called Caldetas, just outside of Barcelona. Our trip took us through Switzerland again—through Geneva, overnight in Lyon, then to France, and into Spain. The hotel entertained our group with a sangria party upon our arrival. We went to the bull fights in Barcelona, and I believe that will be my only one, as one was enough for me. I did not like that. We toured Barcelona. We went to the beach every day and attended a flamenco dancing performance at Costa del Sol—that performance was excellent. The roof of the auditorium was closed for the performance and was opened during the intermissions. I thoroughly enjoyed this, as there was dancing for everyone during the intermissions, and I took pictures of it. I felt comfortable in Spain, because the Spanish influences there are similar to the Spanish influences that can be found on the island where I lived in the Caribbean, as Spain ruled the island for over three hundred years before the British defeated them.

In June, our car was slated to be shipped to Canada, and because of my husband's back problem, the military doctors did not want him to drive long distances in short amounts of time, therefore, it was shipped to Winnipeg, Manitoba, one province over from Saskatchewan, which was our final destination. My husband was given three days to get there instead of the usual one.

Our apartment in Germany was to be painted, so we had to move temporarily into another apartment. Therefore, the packers and movers came earlier to pack and move our boxes. We came to Germany with nine boxes, and now we were leaving with thirteen, along with two crates for our paintings and the sports equipment we had acquired there. I got cleaners in to clean my appliances and my floors when the painting was completed. The military inspectors came to march us out, as the saying goes. We were approved, and was able to move out. We moved to stay at a hotel for one week before we left on our flight to Canada. I had been planning to go to London that week but could not, as I had bronchitis. Our friend, the French liaison officer, invited us to celebrate Bastille Day on the French military base. We witnessed their military parades and their celebrations. This was very impressive, as we were among the French and Russian dignitaries. Les was dressed as a civilian. It was still the time of the cold war, and security among the various military personnel was top priority.

1. My father with his sisters and his parents
2. Me at age 16
3. Les and the children in Germany
4. Les and the children in Bavaria
5. Les and me at party
6. Les and me in Germany

1.   Me in Rome
2.   Les and me at the Vatican
3.   Me in Capri
4.   Les and me at Acropolis – Greece
5.   Me in Mycenae
6.   Les giving me poppy flower

1.   Me at Versailles
2.   Les, me and the children at Innsbrook
3.   Me and the children in Holland
4.   At the Bull Fights in Barcelona – Spain
5.   Flamenco Dancing – Spain

1. My parents home on the island
2. My paternal grandmother and my brother
3. Me at age 2
4. My maternal grandparents
5. My mother
6. My Father

12

RETURN TO CANADA

We left for Canada, as planned; flew to Trenton, Ontario; stopped overnight; and left the next day for Winnipeg. At three o'clock in the morning, the children were awake and requested breakfast—because of the time change, they were hungry. Our flight to Winnipeg took us through Ottawa. We landed in Winnipeg, got a hotel, ate lunch and supper, and then rested our weary bodies. There were so many things that appeared different to me. It seemed that the slices of bread had grown since we left—they were huge. We just were so accustomed to the small slices we'd had in Germany for three years. Our bread, our food, and everything had always been "normal," but now we could not eat the amount of food that was served to us. The following day Les picked up our damaged car—the steering wheel was damaged, as someone had tried to steal it, and the hubcaps were missing—and then we were on our way to Saskatchewan, where he'd been transferred. We would need to take the car to a dealer at our destination, and the military would pay for the repairs, as well as the insurance company.

Because Les was given three days travel time to get to Saskatchewan, we stopped overnight in Brandon, where two of our children were born. Les had spent about eight years at the military base just outside Brandon, where we'd lived in Canada as newlyweds. I first started to work in Brandon. We spent two days and two nights there, visiting people we once knew, including our old landlord and landlady. We continued on to Moose Jaw the following day and got in late in the afternoon. We checked into the same hotel where we'd stayed before leaving for Germany, and they remembered us. We chose that hotel because of the waterslide, the pool, and other facilities for the children. We phoned our friends; they were so surprised because we did not tell anyone we were coming back—we wanted to surprise them. Soon, they all crowded into our hotel suite. My best friend, with whom I had corresponded religiously, did not even know we were coming back. I wanted to surprise her, too.

We did not have to prepare any of our meals, as we were invited out— Guyanese food from my best friend, Jamaican food from another friend, Chinese food from another, and Canadian food from yet another friend. Our priest was also on that list. Fr. Rogers went into the priesthood after he had been in the military, and had fought in World War II. He was an avid hunter. I have to laugh because the children could not pronounce his name, so they called him Father "Ripplefinger." He was good. He officiated at the holy sacraments for both Melani and Leslie, and he officiated at my baptism into the Catholic faith years before. My husband was Catholic; now we were all Catholics, although I had been attending that faith for years. I first went with Deiter Chabot, who was Catholic also.

Les reported for duty. He was assigned to train all pilots on the ejection seats. In the event of an accident or an airplane malfunction, the pilots had to know how to eject from an airplane in flight. I think he liked his job—it changed from a lot of activity to less activity. He started at 7:30 AM and finished at 3:30 PM. Now, we had to find a home. Did we want to buy right away? What should we rent, if and when we built a new home, which we were leaning toward? I was not too amused when I passed the home we had built and sold before we left for Germany. I knew the owners were not about to sell it back to us; they liked it. We ended up renting a brand new house, one street over, and we had to pass our old house every day. This did not make me too happy.

The children returned to their old schools. Jamie, however, started grade one there, and for a while, I returned to being the proverbial housewife, kissing and waving good-bye to husband and children, cleaning house, providing meals, and doing the entertainment thing. By October of that year, I was hired by the provincial government, social services department, to work as a bookkeeping-machine operator. I paid foster parents for keeping children in their care. This was a huge job, as there were many checks produced for the entire province, which was large, and I was the only operator. Once again, I was working in finance.

I left by bus at 7:00 AM for the provincial capital, and returned by 6:00 PM. Les dropped me off at the bus depot and picked me up on my return. We were home for dinner by 6:30 PM, as I had it all prepared. It only needed to be warmed up, which Les and the children did. The military base for which I worked before I left for Germany got wind of my return, and my old boss tried to woo me back, but I had to turn him down. I had moved on to something bigger.

We lived in Saskatchewan from July 1981 to September 1983. It was as if we just picked up our old life again but without our own house. Les was invited to his college reunion so we all went. It was an entire weekend of festivities. We stayed with Les' aunt Beatrice, who was also his godmother. He loved her, and so did she him. We often went to see her, and she us. Friday night was meet-and-greet, and then Saturday for the families, and Saturday night was a dance. Sunday was a family Mass.

Most of his classmates were there. Some I already knew, and others I met for the first time. Some had become priests, and Les marvelled at how the worst and most troublesome of boys could become leaders of men and their souls. They all were absolutely funny.

The college was a Catholic boy's college for high school boys, and after grade twelve they went on to first year of university. They had an excellent academic record. Some went on to university, some to the military, like Les and his best friend, John Bennett. Some went into the priesthood, and most went into their parents' business of farming.

Les went on to the university, to survey school. He had already spent three years in the military as an airborne infantryman and was stationed in Germany. On his return, he left the military and went surveying. He has surveyed most of the highways in Saskatchewan. Because surveying was seasonal in those days, he decided to re-enlist in the military and was shipped off to join the Corps of Army Engineers, building bridges, etc., and training officer cadets. He was then shipped off to the Middle East for a year and a half. This is my story, but he would have a lot to tell about his life—a very fascinating life.

Saskatchewan, however, was just another stop for us. We entertained a lot—many dinner parties at our home, and we attended many in return. As military people, we had friends all over Canada and all over the world.

In the summer of 1982, Les' brothers, Carl and Ted, came to visit us. Carl and his family came back for Christmas. In 1983, we had lots of company from the island, as my brother and his son came to spend a month with us. The daughter of Les' best friend, Denton, got married. Les was the master of ceremonies, and Melani was a bridesmaid, so we all attended.

13
RETIREMENT, LOSS, AND MARRIAGE

In August 1983, Les decided to retire from the military after twenty-nine years and found employment as a civilian. He opted to go back to school to do courses in power engineering. He actually took that job so the children could finish high school and also university. He worked there for twelve years. I also got employment with the government and was to start work in October 1983. We moved from Saskatchewan to Calgary in September 1983 and bought a home in an area where all the schools were available for the children—high school for Melani, junior high for Leslie, and public school for Jamie.

Our children started school in the Catholic system, but in Calgary, they all attended the public system, and they found it very different. Later, Jamie was the only one who went back to the Catholic system for both junior high and high school.

We lived in south-western Calgary for two years. I learned that my best friend in Saskatchewan was diagnosed with cancer. She had sent us a gift for Christmas. It came early, and I waited until Christmas Day to open it, and in that gift was her letter, telling me about her illness. I was devastated. So, off we went to Saskatchewan to visit her.

In 1985, we sold our home in the southwest and moved into interim lodgings while our new house was being built. We then moved in December 1985. It was just a gorgeous house. Moving day was bad, as there was a blizzard and lots of snow. Christmas that year was special. We had lots of our friends over. We went out for New Year's Eve and had company over for New Year's Day.

In the summer of 1986, my best friend and her husband came to visit. She had had an operation earlier in the year for breast cancer, and she appeared to be over the worst. Les and I had been to see her in the hospital earlier. It was so good to see them. We had so much fun while we lived in Saskatchewan. My best friend and I shared the same birthday, January 9, and we always had so much to talk about.

That summer, Melani graduated from high school with scholarships from Alexander Rutherford, the Department of National Defence, and the Royal Canadian Legion. She was accepted at the University of Calgary in the fall of 1986.

On New Year's Eve 1986, we attended a New Year's Eve ball at the military base. We took Melani with us to give her a break from her studies. We went with friends—Neal, who provided the music for the ball, and his wife, Lacey. Melani was introduced to a few of the young men, and as a parent, I could see the immediate interest in her. Larry was the last one she met, and he got most of her dances and her attention. He asked for her permission to come over to visit her.

He appeared to be a very nice young man, and Les gave him the once over, with questions from one military man to another. Larry appeared to be trustworthy; he was originally from Newfoundland.

In the summer of 1987, Les, Jamie, and I went to Saskatchewan to visit friends. My best friend was in the hospital again, due to the cancer that had plagued her earlier. Leslie went to Jamaica to visit my family; Melani stayed home, as she was working for the summer. When we got back from our holidays, my sister phoned to let us know that our father was very sick and was told that he had only six months to live. That news really took the wind out of my sails, and preparations were made as soon as we could to go home to see my father.

Les was to go to Quebec City for meetings, and I was supposed to go into the hospital for an operation, so we tried to arrange our Jamaica trip around that. I postponed my operation in order to go. We went for ten days. It was a very sad and rough trip. My father was sick; he'd also had a stroke and had to be hospitalized. He was released two days later with a cylinder of oxygen, which made it easier for his breathing. It was very difficult to leave him to go back to Canada. Les went to Quebec on our return, and when he came back, I went in the hospital to have the operation I had earlier postponed. I had a ten-week recuperation period.

A telephone line was finally installed in the area where my parents were living, and they had a telephone installed in their home, so I would phone my father every Sunday to see how he was. The last Sunday that I spoke to my father, his speech was inaudible. He talked non-stop, but I did not understand what he said. I just kept telling him that I loved him. Later that evening, my sister phoned to tell me that our father had died. I had been out of the hospital less than a month after my operation. Now, we had to get a flight to the island. The airline was on strike, and I had to get permission to travel. My doctor gave the okay, although I had to be wheelchair-bound. Les' friend, who was a travel agent, had a flight ready for us the following morning. On the way to the airport, we picked up our tickets to catch a flight with Delta Airlines from Calgary to Salt Lake City to Atlanta. We stayed overnight in Atlanta, then on to Miami, and Jamaica the following day. That was a trip. It was good to be home, but at the same time, sadness engulfed my mind and body. My father would be missing. He always picked us up from the airport whenever we went to the island.

It was an emotional ten days spent there. All five of us children, with our spouses, were there. My parents' home was just not the same; the absence of my father left a big void, and my mother appeared to be lost. It was Christmastime.

Les and I went back to Canada via the same route, except for the overnight stay in Atlanta. We got home on December 23. Last-minute shopping had to be done in preparation for Christmas. My mother spent Christmas with my sister and her family at their home.

In January 1988, I returned to work after being absent for over ten weeks. I was not quite well, but my "general illness" time was up, and I felt that I needed to get back to be among people again. I received a call from the husband of my best friend, telling me that Les and I should come to Saskatchewan because she was not doing so well. Les and I flew there to spend the weekend with her. When I was leaving, she gave me such a tight hug. We talked about so many things. She passed away about a week later. I missed her; she was such a lovely person. My children were upset, and I overheard my youngest, Jamie, talking to himself in the mirror in his bathroom. "I asked you not to take Grandpa, and you did not listen, and now I asked you not to take Mrs. Benoit, and you did not listen again." My heart went out to my son, and I gave him a big hug to comfort him.

This was the year, 1988, that Leslie graduated from high school. He was one of thirteen applicants out of over one hundred who was accepted to enter officer training. He was also accepted into the engineering program at the University of Calgary. He then joined the Naval Reserves, went back for more training, passed, and was the recruiting officer for his unit. In 1989, he went back for more training as a maritime engineering officer, at which time he also received the Queen's Commission as a regular force officer. We all went to his graduation and then to visit Les' best friend, Denton, and his mother on Victoria Island. That summer, the entire family was together.

First, Les and I went to Cuba to celebrate our twenty-fifth wedding anniversary. We arrived home on a Sunday. The following day, Monday, we drove out to Victoria for Leslie's graduation. The following day after the graduation we went up Victoria Island, spent a few days, then left to get back to Calgary. We arrived late at night, and the following day, we were on our way to see friends in Saskatchewan, where we spent a few days. Then we came back home to Calgary. That was a lot of traveling.

Earlier that year, Leslie brought a girl, Karen, home to introduce her to us.

For New Year's Eve 1989, Les and I took the children with us to the Carriage Inn to celebrate the evening. Jamie was still underage, so he could not join us. Les and I left early, right after midnight, for home, so we could spend some time with Jamie. Leslie and Karen and some friends left early, so did Larry and Melani. It was not long after we got home that Larry and Melani followed. They looked so nervous. Larry spoke up to Les and asked him for our blessing, because he had asked Melani to marry him, and she had said yes. There was silence, and for the first time in twenty-six years, Les appeared to be at a loss for words. The first thing that he finally said was, "What about her university?" Larry quickly told him that they were going to wait until after she completed her degree to get married. . She was majoring in bio-chemistry, as she had thought that she might go into medicine and therefore wanted to have the prerequisites in the event that she made that decision. Les gave them our blessings and then opened a bottle of champagne to congratulate and celebrate the event. My child was going to become a woman. We were always the best of friends. We two girls in the house were surrounded by three men who had an overabundance of testosterone.

In the summer of 1990, Larry was transferred overseas to work at the Canadian Embassy. He felt it would be best, as Melani was in her final year at university and needed to concentrate. He came home at Christmas, and after her exams, she joined him in Newfoundland to meet his family. Leslie went to Nova Scotia to spend Christmas with Karen's family. Friends of ours, Matthew and Dora Blackeyes, and their daughter came to spend Christmas with us.

In January 1991, Larry was transferred to the Canadian Embassy in Tokyo and wanted Melani to join him, as a gift to her for completing her degree. Her final exam was in April, and after much deliberation, Les finally consented. He had felt that they would get married there, instead of here, in Canada. So said, so done—Larry phoned to tell us their plans that they had decided to get married in Japan, and also told us that they would have another wedding when they got home, as we had been planning. We sent the clothing Melani requested. Les was disappointed because he had wanted to give her away.

Melani was scheduled to return sooner, but Larry extended her ticket so he could have her for another week. She came home just in time for her convocation. Larry came home in July. They had been married in a civil ceremony, and then in the Anglican Church overseas. Melani, who is Catholic, wanted their marriage blessed in her church, so she had her wedding as she had planned when they got home. That went very well, with a reception for friends and family at the Carriage Inn. That, too, was lovely. They then both left from the reception for Labrador via Newfoundland, where Larry was now transferred.

In Newfoundland, Larry's parents and family had another wedding reception for them. Later that year, my sister phoned to say that my mother was sick, and I had to go home to the island, so Jamie and I went. Les could not go, as he had meetings to attend. That Christmas, Leslie went to Halifax and then brought Karen home for New Year's. Larry and Melani came home in 1992 for holidays and to see their wedding gifts that they did not have a chance to see before they left.

14

MORE LOSS

In September 1993, I started four years of courses in social work at Royal Mount College. I only did that so our office and the college would have the necessary numbers to have the course put on, especially for interested government employees. I had fully intended to drop out after the diploma course was approved and I had done the first few months. I am from the financial field and was not really interested in social work. Well, I did not drop out, and in 1997, I was the first one in my class to graduate with a diploma in social work from the college. I really worked hard and took spring and summer courses to get through.

In 1994, Larry and Melani moved to Winnipeg and bought their first house. Larry was accepted into the management program at the University of Manitoba but could not attend due to military commitments. Melani was also accepted at the University of Manitoba to pursue another degree, this time in human ecology. Her ultimate goal was still medicine. We all went to Winnipeg to see them and help them set up their house. I liked their house; it was warm and cozy.

That same summer, the doctor told Les that his sugar level was high, that he was diabetic, and that he should lose some weight. That fall, Jamie started at the University of Alberta in a political science program. Larry and Melani were to come home for Christmas but could not, as Larry's brother and his children were going to be there for Christmas. So, we all decided to go to Winnipeg instead. Leslie drove, and Les, Jamie, and I flew in.

Les lost a lot of weight and was not feeling so good, so on his return to Calgary, January 1995, he went to see the doctor; everything seemed worse. He was sent to the hospital to see an internal specialist and was put on insulin right away. This worked for a while, as he began to feel better, but this was short lived, as he became sick again, and this time, had to be admitted to the hospital. After several tests, he was told that there was a mass on his pancreas, that news left me frozen, and everything went downhill from there. I was devastated. We both cried, and Les worried over what would happen to me. Imagine—he did not think of his own impending doom.

He was operated on, but nothing could be done because of where the mass had spread. The biopsy came back negative, and that is what he was told. The doctor told me that he needed to see Les in the next six months, to see if the mass had grown any. I was happy with that news, because that meant he was all right for another six months, as my own doctor had given me news of dark, dark doom.

I hated every doctor that Les saw or had seen. Our family doctor headed the list because I felt that he should have known in time to help Les, as Les religiously did his annual checkups. Besides, he scared the life out of me when he told me what could happen. Then, perhaps the military doctors should have been more diligent because Les did have some stomach problems when we got back to Canada from Germany. When he retired from the military, he had lost a ton of weight, but we thought it was the change of lifestyle from all his years of regimentation. He hated going to the doctor, like most men, but he did go. He did regain the weight, and it settled around his stomach. Now, life and sickness just stared us right in the face, but the big "C" word never entered our vocabulary. The day he phoned me to say everything went black around him, and when he went to the doctor and was told that he should lose some weight, as his sugar level was high, was the day that our sorrows began. When he was told about the mass on his pancreas, everything went downhill from there, now life and sickness just stared us right in the face.

I had my husband with me for another six months. During that time, we talked a lot, but I did not want to talk about the inevitable, because I was in deep denial, and I refused to think otherwise. I was hoping that he'd get better—people sometimes got very sick and then they began to get better. Until then, no doctor told him that he had cancer. I saw my husband slowly getting sicker. I took him to several of his appointments, and still, nothing was said. The last thing we heard was after his biopsy in January—they could find nothing. They put him on a female cancer drug to see if the mass on his pancreas would shrink, but this appeared to do nothing. I took time off from my place of employment and stayed home with him to ensure that he was taken care of. I took him out driving every day, and we went for long walks every day. The only time I was away from him was to attend the classes I had been taking, and that was for about an hour and a half, twice a week.

Les and I talked a lot, as we had always done throughout our marriage. He felt he was always right, as I let him believe that. Now, we talked about what could be happening to him, but still, I was in denial. He told me that he was sorry for all the times he'd made me mad, when he knew he was the one that was wrong. He told me that he did not want me to live alone, and that I should get married again. One of the funniest things he said, which baffled me for the longest time, was when he said, "Now you can marry your doctor." I had no idea who or what he was talking about, but I came to realize, several years later, that he was talking about Deiter Chabot. He told me just how much he loved me and that he'd had a good life and a good wife that loved him. He had a good home and three wonderful children. What more could he ask for? He called the boys to tell them that he was not going to be here much longer and that they were to take care of their mother. Melani was already married and was living in Winnipeg.

On one of our walks, he asked me what I would do if he was no longer here with me. I did not want to respond, as I just knew that he *had* to be here—he'd promised me that we were going to grow old together, and he could not leave me. I was not going to let him go. He had never promised me anything that he did not deliver. I cried a lot. I tried to hide so he would not see me cry, but he did, and he knew the pain I was feeling. I loved him; I hugged him; I kissed him; I lay beside him. All the time I was optimistic, I was in deep denial. Six months from the day of his operation—July 26, 1995—he was gone. I was devastated and had difficulty accepting this.

Throughout our marriage, we wrote many letters to each other, and my favourite letter from him to me still warms my heart. It read:

> Dearest Marcey,
>
> Why do I want to go on living with you? Well, without you, honey, there is no life, only existence. … You are the end-all and the be-all of me. Without you, I would be nothing but one empty shell. You are my conscience, my heart, my feeling, my brain, and everything that is worthwhile. Honey, you make me operate. You are like the fuel for the machine; without it, I could not run … as I can't even imagine life without

you … you are my heart and I love you so very much. So what are my reasons for wanting to go on living with you? Well, there are no reasons except … you are me; without you, there would be no me. So you see, honey, that I need you and want you for every reason there is but mostly for the most important one, life itself.

All my love.

I still cry when I read this.

By this time, I was halfway through my social work diploma and was about to give it all up, but when I thought of the encouragement Les had given me, I continued, and graduated with a diploma in social work. He had been looking forward to attending. I was devastated for years, and I still am.

I had been off work, as I'd stayed home to be with my husband. I went back, and walked into problems at work. It was like walking into a hornet's nest. I had to fight my battles to survive. Jamie was now home, as he did not want to continue at the University of Alberta. He went to Mount Royal College. It was good to have someone home, as Leslie was in Victoria, and Melani was in Winnipeg. They phoned me every night. They remained with me for quite a while, until Leslie had to return to his military duties, and Melani had to go back to Larry and university.

I got into the role of financial benefits worker from my role as business manager. I was now doing social work. I had a caseload of 345 clients, and I practically had to learn the role on my own, as my miserable co-workers told me that no one was going to show me how to do it. I survived, though, and got many accolades. I liked challenges. Our office also moved to another location to work with the federal workers. The department now had a new name. I then moved to Student Finance and then to Advanced Education and Career Development.

In 1997, I went to Saskatchewan to attend the wedding of my friend's son. They were from Italy, and she, who became my sister, told me that she was not asking me to come to Italy; she just knew that I was coming. In July 1997, I sold my house and was building another—a smaller house I thought, but it turned out to be the same size as the one I had sold. Once again, I had interim lodgings while my house was being built.

15
TRIP TO ITALY

I left for Italy on December 20, 1997. I spent Christmas and New Year's with my friend and her family in Italy. It was just a great trip. I set off early in the morning from Calgary and flew to Toronto. I had a long layover, so my cousins in Toronto came to the airport to pick me up, and I spent the day with them until my flight to Italy, late in the evening.

The man in the seat next to mine struck up a conversation with me, but I really did not want to talk, as my whole system was focused on what lay before me at the end of this plane ride to the Fiumicino Airport in Rome. I was then to get on a train, and then get on a bus, and my ultimate destination was a place called Vasto, about three hours from Rome. The man next to me did not know where that was either.

The next seven to seven and a half hours were uneventful. I kept looking out the windows to see if dawn was breaking. Finally, I saw the sun over the horizon. Well, I was sure glad I'd brought along some books to read, as I did not hear English again (or so it seemed) until I asked where I had to take the Metro train to Rome, and even then I had to listen very closely, to the directions I was being given as my poor language sure sounded different.

The plane seemed to stop in the middle of nowhere. The passengers all got off the plane and then got into what appeared to be a streetcar. We all stood—there were no seats—as we were driven to the terminal.

It was now a race for space in the line-up to get to customs. About three other aircrafts had come in, and we were all shuffling for a space, although it seemed as though everyone was making his own line. But why was I complaining? The island is no different, except for the heat there and the heavy winter coats here.

Finally, a door opened. I followed others who had broken the line to go through this door. They checked my passport and finally, I was on the "other side." I just followed along and came to an area where there was more mass confusion, and I was at the right spot to get my luggage. After what seemed like an eternity, my luggage appeared. I took it off the conveyor and struggled to put it on a cart. I now needed to find out where to get the Metro. I found it, after much asking, and bought my ticket to Piazza Tiburtina—it cost seven thousand lire—and waited for the train.

I figured it would be easy to roll my suitcase on the train, as I thought it would be like our rapid transit in Calgary. No such luck; there were three very steep steps to get up into the train. I could have cried, but I struggled and finally managed to get my suitcase on this train. By now, I really felt that I was going to cry, but I struggled on. This was the very first time I was traveling on my own in a country where the people did not speak English.

The train dumped me at Tiburtina. I'd thought this would be out in the country somewhere—no one had told me, and I was only following instructions—but it was a piazza in Rome. At Tiburtina, I tried to find the bus company but could not. Talk about frustration—no one knew any English. I had to cross two very busy roads and just about got killed dodging cars—those little matchbox things (I was really mad)—to get to the side of the street where the buses were. I finally found a little hole in the wall where the tickets were sold. The fare to Vasto was thirty-seven thousand lire. Now to find the bus—but there was no bus, and no one spoke English, my blessed language. I really did not know where to go. I kept walking back and forth with my awfully heavy suitcase. I even asked a priest, who one would think would at least know English, but he spoke Spanish. He told me to stay where I was; good thing I did not, or I still would have been standing in Tiburtina.

I got upset and frustrated—I hated this place. I just marched myself, heavy suitcase and all, back to the ticket office and asked where was I to go to get the bus to Vasto. God sure works in mysterious ways. There was a middle-aged man buying a ticket, and he'd heard my question in English. He turned to me and said, "Don't worry. I am taking that bus, and I will take you there.—He could have led me anywhere. I followed him.

Three buses were all going to Vasto. The man showed his ticket to one driver, and the driver pointed to the next bus; the next driver pointed to the next bus. Now this was fun and games, as all the buses had Vasto as their destination. I got on the first bus. We set off for Vasto, only to be told in the middle of the Autostrade—the motorway—that that I had to change buses. I did set foot on the Autostrade, where only the rubber from tires had trod. I transferred my luggage to the new bus, and off I went. I now left everything to fate. *Who the heck knows where I was going?* I thought. Only God, because the bus driver obviously did not know.

My discomfort grew greater because after I left the airport at Fiumicino, I did not see another bathroom. The last one was on the plane. I tried every possible thing to not think of what I wanted to do, and I hoped the bus would make a rest stop so I could get off and do my thing. No, there were no rest stops, so for seven hours, my discomfort grew by the minute.

After three hours on the bus, and I actually arrived at Vasto. I was comforted to see my friends; there was a nice, big welcoming party for me. I was happy. I went in one car, and my suitcase went in another, because it could not fit in the Italian Fiat cars. When we got home, another welcoming party was there, but you know what I had to do—I could not even talk. By this time I had accumulated gallons of water that I just had to get rid of. I also realized that I had not eaten since I was served breakfast on the plane, and it was now after seven in the evening.

It was good to finally stop my travels and hear some English. I had lost a whole day, and I was really tired. After the company left, I had a shower—the last time I'd had one was at 6:30 AM the day before, at my own home in Canada. It was refreshing. I slept like a log until after nine o'clock the next morning. The others had been up and had gone to church and were now back.

My fifteen-day visit was really wonderful, even though the weather was damp and cold—it was December, but there was no snow. I had to go shopping for warmer clothing, as the dampness was uncomfortable. Calgary's weather is cold but dry in December. During my visit I went to my friend's childhood home, traveled over the countryside, and went to see the home and monastery where Father Pio, the monk who was soon to be canonized by the Pope, had lived. He was the monk whose hands bled as if there were nail prints in the palm of his hands, but there were no visible scars. I attended Mass in the beautiful chapel there, where there was standing room only. I visited Father Pio's tomb in the basement of the church, as well as the room where he lived—that was very interesting. I saw the Stations of the Cross and the beautiful hospital that was built near the monastery from donations given by the faithful.

I went to Mass every morning while I was in Italy. Christmas was great, as I learned about the Italian traditions at Christmastime. There are hardly any Christmas trees, but just about every home that I visited had a Nativity scene. The churches displayed very elaborate Nativity cradles, as they are called. I visited with all the brothers and sisters of my friends— they were a family of nine siblings. Their meals were scrumptious, and their homes were beautiful.

New Year's Eve was very entertaining. I did learn to speak some Italian. A party was held, and all the family attended. I think I put on some weight while I was there; it seemed as if I was eating all the time—pasta in all different forms and Italian bread.

It was now January 5, 1998, and it was time to go back to Canada and home. I boarded the bus for Tiburtina and of course, I needed to go to the bathroom. This time the bus made a rest stop, and I was happy.

At Tiburtina, my second encounter with this city, I had to walk across the busy streets again and pull my suitcases down two flights of stairs. Because of my shopping, I had to buy myself another suitcase. Now, I had three suitcases, two to be checked, and one hand luggage. I got them on a cart, only to find another flight of stairs around the corner, this time to get up to the platform. Off came my suitcases from the cart, and not for the life of me could I get them up the stairs. God is good, as a nice young man came along, and he lifted the heaviest one up the flight of stairs for me, while I dragged the other two up. I worried the entire time that he might hurt himself. We got to the platform and waited about ten minutes. Once the train arrived, I had to get the suitcases up those narrow steps and on to the train. I nearly fell forward, because the heavy one would not budge. Someone helped me by pushing as I pulled—it was a regular spectacle that we made of ourselves, but we got the suitcases on the train.

I think I lost forty pounds with all that exercise. I was sweating like a little pig, and that darned heavy woollen jacket with a turtleneck sweater under my blouse certainly did not make matters any easier. I rested the suitcases where they landed in the middle of the aisle, and people had to step over them to get on and off the train. *Who cares?* I thought. *They are on.* When I got to the airport at Fiumicino in Rome, I pulled the suitcases down the steps, one at a time, and did not even care if the wheels got broken. I would push them if I had to, in order to get them on the plane. I found a cart and loaded my suitcases on them and went into the airport. No more steps. I could not believe it. After a long ramp, I was there at Departures. I could hardly wait to check my suitcases in. It was not difficult to find the Canadian ticket area, and I made a beeline for it with my cart. I was tired, and I was hot. I checked my suitcases through to Calgary. Well, that was the end of that. Little did I know that I would have to retrieve them in Toronto, go through customs, and then put them through again for Calgary. I got to Calgary after my long return flight, but lo and behold, my suitcases had been left in Toronto. They did arrive on a later flight, but that meant that I had to hang around the airport until they came in. I finally got home at 12:30 AM. Because my friend had been diagnosed with breast cancer and not very well, my trip to Italy had been necessary.

16
SOLILOQUY

In 1998, I graduated from the University of Calgary Continuing Education with a certificate in career development. In December 1998, my friend died in Italy. She had phoned me one last time to tell me good-bye and said that I should not cry but just think of all the good times and laughter we'd shared. I was very sad.

I then decided to get a degree in social work, so I applied to the University of Victoria's Bachelor of Social Work Program, and I was accepted. I also changed my place of employment to the federal office but still worked as a provincial employee. In 1997, I had sold my house and built another; I moved in January 1998.

In 2000, Jamie and I went to spend Christmas and New Year's in Toronto with my cousin Zickle and her family. In 2001, I went back to Toronto to see my last remaining uncle, who was very sick and in the hospital. I went back again later in the year for his funeral. In 2002, I went to Toronto again for the fiftieth wedding anniversary of another cousin, Darlene, and her husband, Sam.

In June 2003, Jamie got married; it was a very nice wedding. In July, my best friend's husband passed away. I could not attend the funeral because I went with Larry and Melani to Newfoundland, to his sister's wedding and to meet his family. They were very nice, and I had a great time. From there, I went to Toronto to attend my nephew's wedding. Jamie was the master of ceremonies. I then went back to Calgary to attend the wedding of another dearest friend's daughter. That was lovely. Jamie's daughter, my granddaughter, Riley, was born December 14, 2003. She was absolutely gorgeous. I suggested that I would babysit while they took a break and went out.

At that time in my life, I was content and was happy just living my life. I had resigned myself to not having any relationships, as I had so many memories of my husband and the beautiful life we lived. I loved to cook for the company who came to my house. I love people and had a lot of company. I liked grocery shopping, as I could try the things that I was not too familiar with. I liked going out to eat occasionally and sometimes to a movie with my children and my friends. I also liked quiet times to replenish my energies and my thoughts, and my chesterfield (couch) was one of my favourite spots to listen to music that suited my mood and just reminisce. This took me back to other places, people, and things that I did that gave me pleasure, but it also brought some sadness. Special places also are places of historical facts and sights. Special places were in my parents' home. I loved my parents. I did not always see eye to eye with them when I was much younger, but they became so very smart when I grew up.

Now, I still love to travel. I love archaeology and anthropology. I will either read or watch documentaries on the television about people before me and in my time. I find that fascinating, especially when I think of all the old civilizations that I am walking over every day. I have often said that if I could relive my life, I would either be an archaeologist or an anthropologist. I love nature; I love flowers and all sorts of flowering plants. I also love documentaries on nature and the animals.

My favourite things are found in speciality kitchen and home stores and in the home and kitchen area in all department stores; that is where I go to see what is new. I love dishes and anything in that line that are different. I collect teapots and cups and saucers and have a lot of them. These are really my favourite things. I do not own a china dinner service, because as a wedding present, I got a set of four Jamaican dishes that my husband made into a service of eight for a full dinner service. These dishes have seen a lot of company.

I am not a member of any special clubs, as I don't want to be regimented into any one thing, as I believe it would become a chore. I like to be spontaneous in whatever I choose to do. Driving is not my most favourite thing to do; I like being driven. Now that I am retired and have moved to Nova Scotia, I do enjoy driving from my home into the city. This drive reminds me of the island, driving by the ocean, which for me emotes a feeling of security. On the other hand, my biggest fears at one time were death and dying and the dead. I believe I have since come to terms with that, although there are still some underlying issues. I am also fearful of not having enough resources to enjoy my retirement.

I don't have many heirlooms, but I do have a lemonade set that my father gave to my mother as an engagement present. As a child, I had always admired it and asked if I could have it when I grew up. Well, that is now in my possession, and it is very precious.

After my husband had been gone for about eight years, my friends suggested that I go out with someone to a movie and to dinner, etc. I said that I was not interested, because whoever that person was, he would ask me for things that I was not prepared to give. However, I said that if I did go out with anyone, it would have to be someone from my past who was just a friend and that maybe that friendship could develop into something else.

17

OLD LOVE, NEW FRIENDSHIP

The date was December 27, 2003. My phone rang, and at the other end of the line was a male voice, who said, "This is someone from your past." I was a bit angry at this prank and told him that I did not have much of a past, so who was he? I almost hung up then he told me who he was—Deiter Chabot, my first love from thirty-eight years ago. I lost all control in my legs and had to sit. I was scared; I did not know what he was going to say. I had been told that he was angry with me when I chose to marry Les and had said that I had better not cross his path again. Instead of saying something angry, however, he told me that I was the love of his life. This scared me also, because I did not know how to respond. I told him that I did not know that, because he had never told me, and that I had married a wonderful man.

I then asked how he'd gotten my number. And I asked how all our friends were doing, as the only person I was in contact with was Cara. She had given him my number, he finally admitted. He told me that he was divorced and had remarried. I made a mental note of that, I did not have time to digest all that he said. I felt euphoric and was almost walking on air at the thought that he had tried so hard to find me, and that he said that he would have never married if he had known that I was alone and single. It was the thought of finding a friend after all these years. I still loved him after all these years. I laughed at our conversation about old times. I was so nervous, I could not stay still. The universe must have heard me say that it had to be someone from my past when my friends told me that I should go out with someone. I was not even thinking about Deiter, because I knew he was married, and I did not want to interfere or get involved.

He gave me his telephone number, and we exchanged addresses. He said he would send me some pictures and he asked me to send some of mine. I phoned Cara, and we just laughed together about all this. I told my children about him, and they teased me. I was so excited, and wondered if he would call again soon. I also felt guilty; it was as though I was cheating on my husband's memory, but then, I felt his presence, and he made me feel that it was all right

On January 9, 2004—my birthday—Deiter called again, but I was out. He called again the next day, and we really talked. Our conversation was emotional, fully confirming that our love for each other was still there and real. He told me that he took full responsibility for what had happened to us, and that he had abandoned me. He told me he had been searching for me for years. I asked him, if he was trying so hard to find me, why did he get married again. I did not feel comfortable with the fact that he was married. He said that if he'd known where I was and had found me, he would have never married. I asked him what he was going to do about this situation, and he said, "It is going to be messy." This gave me hope. I asked no more questions. I knew he loved me; I could feel it, and I could hear it in his voice. His first letter told me how much he had missed me all these years. I loved him, too. Now, I had another issue to deal with. I was trying to finish the last four months toward my degree.

Why on earth had he called me, especially when he was married again? All the old feelings came back. I was vulnerable; I had been alone for a long time, and although I wanted no one in my life, I was ready for this. This was my first love, someone who had been the love of my life. He called often, and it was just great talking to him. We talked about his marriage, and we quarrelled about what he'd made happen to us, although now, he wanted to blame me, which really made me upset. What I found out about him was that his wives knew about me because he told them.—I felt sorry for him. He told me that he was not happy and that he was bored. I didn't know what he wanted me to do. I just knew that I wanted to love him and comfort him, yet at the same time, I didn't want anyone to be hurt. Why had he put the responsibility of what happened in his life on me? We spent many hours on the phone, just talking and laughing and teasing and quarrelling and asking questions as we tried to fill in thirty-eight years of absence and happenings in our lives.

In June 2004, he came to visit and spent five days with me. Deiter and I had been good kids. Our passionate affair then was relegated to kissing each other, and that was the best. I flew to Edmonton to get him and then flew back to Calgary to take him to my home. I was so excited just to touch, hold, and kiss him again. Leslie, Jamie, and Carl, my brother-in-law, came over to meet him. Now, for the second time in my life, I would be behind closed doors with a man, the man who first taught my body to shake and tremble with emotion, those thirty-eight years ago. In the weeks before he came, I searched my soul as to what I should do. I had never made love to any other man but my husband and certainly not outside a marriage. After much labouring over that, I convinced myself that it was all right to make love to him, as he so wanted to love me, and I him. I had mixed emotions, and I was extremely nervous. We spent a lot of time talking. We laughed, we talked, we danced, we loved, we went to Banff, we went for walks, and then it was time for him to leave. I now remembered what my husband had told me when he knew he was dying: "Now, you can marry your doctor." I realized that he might have been talking about Deiter.

The morning before we left my house to go to Edmonton, and in the course of conversation at breakfast, I asked him why did he get married if he did not want to, as he had said before. His response was troubling, as he said, "you don't understand, this is like a business." I did not want to pursue this response as I did not know what else to say, so my next question was what did he and his wife do when they were home. He asked me if I meant what they did when they were not making love. I was taken aback and felt hurt. I began to feel insecure at the response to my question, which I thought was very negative, and it took me by surprise, as I was sitting on his lap. I was a little speechless, because I detected a note of sarcasm. I overlooked it and then moved on.

He then posed the question that he said he thought I wanted to ask: "So, Deiter, where do we go from here." I said, "No, I was not going to ask, but since you brought this up ... so, where are we going from here?" I felt cold. He said he would like to have the option to come back to visit me and see me anytime he could. He said he would like to keep our communication going. And he further said that he did not think it was fair for him to ask me to wait until he decided what he wanted to do with his life and what direction he might want to take. I was too naive to even think that was a line.

My responses were that, without a doubt or a second thought, he was very welcome to come anytime he wished and to stay as long as he wanted. My home, my hospitality, my friendship, and my love were open to and for him. I also answered, without hesitation, that I wanted to keep our communication going. I just had to get used to and understand that it was not always easy for him to call—or for me to call him. I did not respond to the third question which was, he could not ask me to wait for him until he decided what he wanted to do with his life, as I had to think about it.

We flew to Edmonton on the evening before he had to take his flight back to Atlanta the following morning. We then went for dinner and for a walk. That night, I cried most of the night, knowing he would be gone again. I still didn't know where this friendship was going, and I really did not know what I felt. He did not give me any reassurances, so I could not contain my tears. He did tell me that he had never loved anyone as he had loved me. I thought, *how stupid can I be to think that he came to reassure me of our love?*

We kissed; it was like old times, and then I just cried and cried again. We got to the airport, and he had to check in with his luggage to customs and had to leave me. He phoned me from his departure gate, and then he left. Once again, I felt the separation I had felt when he went to university those thirty-eight years ago. I took a flight back to Calgary and went to see my friend Oona.

Deiter called from Phoenix, before he got back to Atlanta. He sounded strange and disconnected from me. He told me that I had changed and that I had become "hard." This I did not understand, so I said, "I am not aware of that, just as long as I don't lose the capacity to love." He said that I had not lost that. I felt a disconnection and real sadness once again. I told him that I was not the same naïve girl that he'd known thirty-eight years ago. I had grown up, but there was still some naivety left in me. At the end of the conversation, there was no warmth. He called me the next Monday night. Our conversation appeared to be going nowhere. The topic again was that I'd run away. I phoned him on Tuesday, and he sounded mean when I asked him, "So where do we go from here?" He got upset and told me that it was the same as he'd said thirty-nine years ago. He also said that he had not asked me to marry him, and nobody was going to make him do anything that he did not want to do. I really did not know what he was talking about—such naivety on my part, and more insecurity; I was crying. He put me on a psychological guilt trip, and I was being drawn into this web. I began once more to reason with myself: *Could he be that cruel?* When he phoned, he would tell me that he would call me—then he never did. When he did, I could hear something like a detachment in his voice that I could not understand. I felt used, and all I could do was cry.

Once again, my questions were not answered. I wished that he'd never called me. I prayed to God to take this all away from me. I had lost Les eight years ago, and that had been difficult, and I could not go through another session of hurt again. My first hurt came from Deiter when he broke my heart. *Please don't let it happen again.* I felt, however, that it *was* happening again, and I did not know what to do. I needed to see him face to face, so he could tell me why his behaviour toward me had changed. I booked a flight to the island in November, with stops, both going and coming, in Atlanta. I thought maybe I should respond to his third question, so the next time he phoned me, I told him that if he had asked me that question thirty-nine years ago, the response would have been the same as I was about to give now: "I will wait. I am not going anywhere, and if it does not work, so be it." This came from my heart.

I got to Atlanta late, as my plane had been delayed in Calgary. I just knew that I had to see him, so that I could ask him all the questions I wanted to ask and to see what had happened. Why had he begun to distance himself from me since he last saw me in Calgary? What had I done? I told him that I had an overnight stop in Atlanta, and he said that he would be at the airport to meet me. He was not there, but he sent Carlene, one of his friends, to meet me to take me to my hotel. It was to be his birthday soon, so I brought him a gift, which I ended up mailing to him from the airport. He phoned me the next morning to say he was sorry and that he was going to try to come down to the hotel. He never came. I was humiliated, and I just cried. While at the airport, I phoned him and read a letter to him that I had written, asking questions and telling him how I was feeling.

On the way back from the island, about ten days later, I had another overnight stop in Atlanta. He said that he would be at the airport to meet me, and once again, he did not show up. He sent Carlene to pick me up again. This time, she did not come up to my room; she just deposited me outside the hotel and then drove off. Once again, I was so humiliated. I had asked her what he was doing that he could not come to meet me. She told me that he'd decided to relax in front of his fireplace. I felt so hurt. The next morning, he phoned, and then he came to see me at the hotel. I was not that happy with his treatment, and I showed it. We talked at length and for some reason, I was so very sad. I left to return to Calgary, and he said he would phone me, which he never did.

Nothing was resolved. Why had he found me? What did he want from me? I felt this newfound friendship was stalling, and once again, I reverted to the sad times I'd experienced in 1964. Lots more tears were shed; I had been used. There had been numerous phone calls before he came to Calgary, then fewer after he came and left, and fewer yet after I saw him in Atlanta. There were a lot of arguments. I really felt like ending this; after all, he had a wife. Why did he continue to call me? I began to feel that he came back into my life because he wanted to punish me for marrying someone else, and that had really messed with his ego. I just felt that I could not turn my back on him because he needed to work through what was eating him inside, and I would be the one to help him through it. He had said that I had wrecked his life when I left him.

It now appeared that every conversation since was a chore. It was always that I'd run away and that I'd hurt him. There was nothing about my being hurt. I felt he had some ulterior motive and a hidden agenda. He told me he had none. I told him I was going to talk to his friend Carlene. He said it was okay. I told her a lot about what he'd done, and what had happened to me when he left, and how I married someone else. We talked for hours. He was giving me another psychological guilt trip, and here I was again, teetering on the verge of another broken heart.

My mother passed away in April 2005, and Leslie and I went to Jamaica. I was gone for over two weeks, as I had to take care of things. I phoned Deiter from the island to tell him that my mother had passed away and that I was to give the eulogy. He gave his condolences and wished me luck.

In May 2005, Leslie and I went to Oregon. It was his gift to me for Mother's Day. It was a nice trip, and I always liked going places with him. Larry and Melani came to live in Calgary. They stayed with me for a while until they could move into their house. Melani had just had my third grandson, and he was a cutie. Deiter's telephone calls still came. He told me that he had seen one of our friends, Frederick, in Florida when he went to his high school Old Boys Association dinner and dance. He gave me Frederick's phone number, and I called him. It was so nice to talk to the man who I'd called my brother.

In 2005, I put my house up for sale, as I felt that moving into a condo was the right thing to do. I sold it to a girl from the island, who had just come to Calgary to work. My cousin Barbara from Barbados came to visit and helped me move into the condo. I soon realized I'd made a mistake; I really did not like it there. I had no space. I had just moved from a four-bedroom house with a basement, etc., and now I was in a two-bedroom condo without a basement, and I did not like it. That year, Larry and Melani had Thanksgiving and Christmas dinners, as I had no space to accommodate the whole family.

18
TRIP TO EUROPE

In December 2005, I went to spend Christmas and New Year's with my sister and her family. It was nice to get away to get some warm weather. Les, my son, (I also called him Les after my husband) was about to change his job and had to use up his vacation days, so early in 2006, he and I went to London, Scotland, Portugal, Spain, and Gibraltar.

The flight to London was eight and a half hours. We landed in the mother country at 2:30 AM Calgary time, which was 9:30 AM London time. We took the express tube to Paddington Station, where we stopped for a coffee and hot chocolate at a coffee shop in the station. I could not believe it, but this place was not heated. I had heard of the heating situation in Britain, but I could not imagine this. We sat in the cold coffee shop as I drank my hot chocolate with my winter jacket on; I watched the pigeons walking all around me and watched workers making sushi, in a Japanese deli nearby. I was in a mall—can you believe that? To me, a mall is enclosed, and it is heated. People were walking all over and shopping. In Canada, I bet the stores would go bankrupt if they had these same conditions.

We then walked from Paddington Station in more cold to find our hotel, which was only about two blocks away. It was cold; I felt I was walking on my knees, as my feet felt frozen, and this was threatening my lower extremities. At the hotel, we could not get into our room until 2:00 PM. We did not want to wait in the lobby y, so we left our luggage in the hotel luggage room, and went back into the cold outdoors, to take a walk in Hyde Park and Kensington Gardens, a few blocks from the hotel.

I was already tired, so I was now doubly frozen and literally felt that my toes had retreated into my ankles. I'd brought no gloves, so I tried to pull my arms up into the sleeves of my jacket, but they popped to the outside often, as I had to wipe my runny nose. I did not like that one bit. It seemed as if we'd been walking for hours; then it was time to go back to the hotel. I have no idea why I complained about the cold. I lived in Germany for three years, and this was the same torture I endured there. The cold weather in London is very damp, and without the proper woollen clothing, a person can be chilled to the bone. Well, I remembered that in a hurry, as I had on a sweater, a pair of jeans, thick rubber-soled walking shoes, and socks—and thanks to Les, I'd brought my thick winter ski jacket, which was my security. I'd been about to take a lighter jacket with me, but he said, "No, Mom, trust me. You had better take a heavier jacket." Truth be told, though, I was fascinated by the park, and its size of 340 acres, and its many statues and ponds. We did a lot of walking.

The hotel at which we stayed was quite nice, but I needed a map to find my way to the elevators, to the restaurant, and to the reception area. It was a real obstacle course. The elevator, however, opened right outside the door to our room, so we had that beat. The heating was provided by steam radiators, and I was very comfortable, because they were at the foot of my bed. There, I was nice and toasty warm, and I really had to force myself out of bed in the mornings, as I wanted to give my feet some comfort after the abuse they had endured from the frozen pavement. The bathroom was a little ancient but good enough—a nice warm shower and a tub. The toilet, basin, and bidet were not quite as lavish, according to North American standards.

We took a rest after our walk in Hyde Park and from being jetlagged. I, for one, felt as frozen as a turd, which I cannot really imagine, but that word seemed appropriate at the time. I slept for about an hour and was up and really raring to go.

We took a night tour of London on one of their double-decker sightseeing buses and made the mistake of sitting on the upstairs (outside) deck of the bus. I was too proud to admit that my eyeballs felt frozen, so I put the hood of my jacket, which I'd never used before, over my head and covered my ears. Then I tried to maneuver the earphones so I could hear the running commentary by the narrator of what sights we were seeing.

I saw some beautiful sights: Trafalgar Square, Piccadilly Circus, St. Paul's Cathedral, etc., all lit up. Piccadilly Circus was just crowded with shoppers, as all the name-brand stores were there. I took note of Liz

Claiborne, as I planned to return there to do some shopping. Obviously, I was too tired to return and felt that my money was better off in my pocket.

Les and I got off the bus at Victoria Station—that was where the driver "dumped" us because his shift was over. And to think here was a "brother" perhaps someone from the island, as there are many Jamaicans living in Britain.—Well, there were lots of "brothers" in London, but as they opened their mouths to say something, that is where the brotherhood and similarities terminated. Their thick British accent was discernable. We took the tube back to Paddington Station, and then went out for dinner. This was entertaining. We went to a Greek restaurant, where I ordered moussaka, which really took a long time to get to us. We ate olives and bread in the interim. There were other patrons in the restaurant, and they were getting very agitated, as their meals were taking some time to get to them. After making a big scene, they refused to pay for the drinks they had consumed. They walked out of the restaurant, with the waiter running after them into the streets to get his money, which he never got. I could hardly contain my laughter. The moussaka was good.

I slept like a log, and the next day we went touring again. Buckingham Palace, among other sites, was a must on our list of priorities. I was not disappointed, as for years I had only seen it on television. It did not, however, stop me from thinking how decadent it was and wondering why the queen needed all that monumental space. Still, I was fascinated. We also visited the Queen's Gallery that displayed the most gorgeous pictures and artefacts. Next on my list was to have a meal of English fish and chips. It made me sick, as it was greasy, and I could not eat it all. That night we went to an Italian restaurant for dinner and ate some more grease, and I was even sicker. I deposited what I'd eaten in the toilet, as it refused to stay in place.

Now it was time to get our flight to Scotland. We flew from Prestwick to Glasgow, and Glasgow was colder than I'd expected. I saw "brothers" living there. I wondered how they did it, and what type of blood ran through their veins. I knew now why Scottish men came to the island; they needed the warmth (and of course to populate the island)—no offence intended here; this is my own opinion, and I am really glad they did, because here I am, one living product. The cold in Glasgow was really very icy and damp. We had planned to take a tour of the city but did not, because the tour bus did not show up. I was glad, as I had no intention of freezing my eyeballs in the twilight of my life, thank you very much.

Shopping was simply out—no fun, too cold—but I did buy myself a pair of woollen gloves to protect my fingers from freezing and ultimately falling off. (Thank God for the sheep that provided this luxury.) The cost of such an item was not a matter of concern in moments like these. I didn't know how anyone could live there. I'd wanted to see the place that was a part of my heritage, but I soon gave up that idea and flew back to London. In fairness, I should say that we went to Scotland in March, a time when winter was still in high gear in Canada.

We left the following morning for Portugal and hoped that it was warmer there. We arrived in Lisbon and took a taxi to our hotel. We then went walking down to the waterfront, as I just needed to see the ocean. It was nice and warm there. It was a long day, and I was glad to get back to the hotel after dinner for a good rest. I can't believe it, but I slept until 10:30 AM, which was so unlike me. I showered, got dressed, and then went for a brunch. I liked Portugal; I felt comfortable there. It was another part of my heritage. We took several bus tours, and we took the train to Porto in the northern part of Portugal—the home of excellent port wines that were exported around the world. This was a three-hour train ride. We spent the day touring Porto and flew back to Lisbon that night.

The next day we went to Cascais, a resort just outside of Lisbon. We took the train and spent the day there—lots of shopping and lots of people. I decided to have some codfish for lunch, as I felt that if any race of people could cook fish, then it had to be the Portuguese. I was not disappointed. I must add that I am not a lover of fish, but this was good.

We had decided to go to a shopping center at Campara, where there was a huge shopping outlet, so after breakfast, we took a cab to get the big bus that was to take us, at no cost, to this shopping center. There were lots of patrons already waiting to get on the bus, and for the first time in Portugal, I saw a lot of disorder—people pushing and stampeding to get on the bus. The poor bus driver was at a loss as to what to do. He was yelling at the crowd, but I don't think they even heard him; they were yelling so much. We did not even try to get on the bus; we just walked back to the shopping center and walked around. It was just strange to see a breakdown in law and order.

The following day, we took a flight to Madrid, Spain. It was Sunday, and we were now in a Catholic country, so I was surprised to see that the stores were open on a Sunday, and there were so many people shopping. We took several bus tours in Madrid, and of course I was so pleased to see the sights and the places of historical importance.

The day after, we flew down to Malaga, rented a car, and drove to Gibraltar. I was impressed with Gibraltar, as it proved to be a very fascinating place. I was mesmerized by the size of the rock that protruded from the ocean, with very little land connecting it to the Spanish mainland. This little country belongs to Britain, so we had to go through immigration. This place was almost surrounded by water, except for the little space that one drives over from Spain. It is a very strategic military base, as British military personnel were stationed there, along with their dependents. The airport and the landing field runs across the highway that enters Gibraltar; consequently, cars and other vehicles cannot cross into Gibraltar if there is landing and taking off of any aircraft. We walked around the sights—all the stores are duty-free, but I did not buy anything. At the end of the day, we drove back to Malaga to get our flight back to Madrid. We were flying back to London in the morning and then back to Canada the morning after.

19
TRIP TO PORTUGAL AND SPAIN

Les' new job with an oil company now entailed a lot of traveling to Europe, so once or twice per month he had to go for meetings there. Later that year, in October 2006, Les was to attend meetings in Portugal. He asked me if I wanted to meet him there. I flew from Calgary to Montreal. I checked my luggage through to Lisbon. My next flight was seven and a half hours to Frankfurt. I got in at 6:30 AM, Frankfurt time. The time difference was seven hours. I was checked through security again, as my flight to Lisbon was to leave at 9:30 AM, and then it would be another two and a half hours to Lisbon by Lufthansa.

Having lived in Germany for three years, I could see that the weather patterns had not changed—it still appeared to be overcast and damp, but then, to be fair, it was early in the morning. Once I got checked in again, I proceeded to my gate. I was so tired and looked like and felt like a wreck. The aircraft got in on time. I then claimed my luggage. There was no customs check, so I proceeded out to meet Leslie—I also called him "Les," after my husband. He had been in Portugal since October 20, attending a conference with another coworker; both were engineers. It was good to see them both. Les felt that I needed a coffee to enjoy one of my favourite Portuguese dainties. I don't know the name, but it is custard or flan in pastry, like a tart—yummy.

We took a taxi to the hotel, where I showered and changed. Then we took another taxi over to a big shopping outlet, as Les' coworker was to catch a flight back to London and Calgary the next morning and now had the opportunity to shop. I could hardly wait to get under the covers; I had gone through three time zones and did not know which end was up. My head had barely hit the pillow when I was in Never Neverland.

We left on our flight the next afternoon for Faro, on the Mediterranean side of Portugal. The scenery was absolutely beautiful—ocean, ocean, and more ocean. Leslie picked up the car he had reserved, and we were on our way to the hotel, which was thirty kilometres outside Faro in a village called Albufeira, and then into a smaller village called Sao Rafael. It was dark by the time we got to the hotel, so I was unable to see the scenery. We checked into our hotel and went for dinner at the hotel restaurant. To my surprise, what I ordered came uncooked—medallions of pork, beefsteak, and lamb. When it appeared, I vowed that I was not going to eat it. The waitress then brought me a cooking stone, and I realized that I had to cook my own meal, and then I had to pay for it.

The following morning, I was awake with the sun. I went on the balcony and there, right in front of my eyes, was the Atlantic Ocean in all its glory. My heart swelled; it is hard to explain to someone who has not grown up in the presence of an ocean or on an island just what this means. Tears came to my eyes. I was so emotional; if I never saw anything else, that was my crowning glory. I was now stationary, the scenery was stable, and now the ocean was mine. I sat on the balcony to absorb some of the air into my lungs and into my pores. I thanked Leslie immensely for his choices.

We decided to drive to the end of the continent to Sao Vincente, where there was nowhere else to go but into the ocean—and it is one sharp, steep, high, killer drop into the ocean. Here the highway ended. A lighthouse marked the point for ships. It was really scary and very windy, with nothing but water all around. I would not, under any circumstances, go too close to the edge, as it would have been a sharp drop-off the end of the earth. My mind turned to the volcanic eruptions that propelled this land from the ocean.

The following morning we drove to Seville, Spain. Seville is an absolutely lovely, historic place. We got there just in time to take one of their bus tours of the city. I learned that this was a Moslem stronghold for over five hundred years. It was discovered by the Phoenicians in 25 BC. Relics of their habitation were plainly visible. It was the center of Moslem power for centuries. The capital of Spain was once Granada, and then it moved to Madrid.

Seville was a major trading area and a big port for years. I saw where Christopher Columbus once lived, where he died, and where he was originally buried. His remains were later moved to Santo Domingo, which is now the Dominican Republic. One of the palaces in Seville is over eight hundred years old, and although it was not a capital, it was the residence of the royal family throughout the centuries. Seville has always been a trading place; hence, several trading houses were visible. Bach and Mozart wrote songs for operas and plays about it; and Rossini wrote *The Barber of Seville.*

Moslem, Jews, and Christians coexist to this day. There were tons of orange trees lining the boulevards. I was at home with the vegetation, as all the shrubbery, the flowers, the trees, and other plants are visible on the island where I had lived. The hibiscus plant, which is the national plant and flower of the island, are visible all over. Because my island home was inhabited and ruled by Spain for over three hundred years, I believe it is obvious that the conquerors brought many of their artefacts with them. The weather in Seville was 29°F (32°C), and that was October, whereas in Calgary at the same time, it was -10°F and snowing. Here, I got a suntan and was so proud of myself. We drove back to our hotel and were to leave for Lisbon the following evening. Therefore, the only constructive plan for the following day was packing our suitcases to fly back to Lisbon, where we were to spend a few more days, then to get on our flight to London, and then on to Calgary.

Our plane from Lisbon was late in leaving, so we got to London late and eventually missed our connection to Calgary. We had to be rerouted later to Ottawa and got home later that night. It was good to be home, but I discovered in Ottawa that I had no luggage—it had not left Portugal. I did, however, get it delivered to me a few days later, all intact, with my house keys still sitting at the bottom where I had put them. I was lucky that I lived in a condominium complex, so one of my neighbours let me in. I had given a set of my house keys to each of my children, so I got a set of keys from Les.

20

RETIREMENT—MOVE TO NOVA SCOTIA

In March 2007, I came to Nova Scotia to see my best friend, Oona. She encouraged me to move there, as I was thinking of retiring from my job. I enjoyed my visit with her; she was my dearest friend and sister. Deiter called me on my cell everywhere I went. His calls came every day, sometimes twice per day. I was glad to hear from him, and our calls were long and interesting. He told me that he was coming to Nova Scotia when I moved there. I was happy and started looking forward to his visit. From there, I went to Barrie, Ontario, to see if I would rather move there instead.

I fell in love with Nova Scotia, so I returned in July to find a home to buy. I bought a house overlooking the ocean. With that done, my friends and I took a trip to Prince Edward Island and that was enjoyable. It was so beautiful there. I went back to Calgary to sell my condo. I came back to Nova Scotia in September to take possession of my house, although that did not take place until October 1, 2007. On that day, Oona and I bought a houseful of furniture, as I did not intend to ship all the stuff I had in Calgary. In December, I came to Nova Scotia again to receive the furniture and effects that I had shipped from Calgary.

My condo was sold in October, and I went to stay with Jamie until I retired and moved to Nova Scotia. In February 2008, I came back to Nova Scotia and stayed in my house because of insurance purposes. Oona was told by her doctor, an oncologist that she had about a year to live; she was diagnosed with leukemia. This was not a very pleasant time for her, and she was upset. We phoned another dear friend in Calgary, Karmen, to get some words of wisdom from her, as Oona had been crying a lot. A few days later, I went back to Calgary and to my job as a career consultant. I had hoped to retire in May 2008, but I was talked out of it, so I came back to Nova Scotia in May. I noticed that Oona was not feeling too well and had to be in her bed, "horizontally," as she would call it. Some days she was up; some days she was horizontal. I went back to Calgary and back to work with the hope of retiring in October. I just could not make it another month. I was simply burnt out, so I decided to put in my retirement request, to retire September 15, 2008, instead of October 31, and my last day of work would be August 29, 2008.

In June, Oona went to Turkey to see her mother. She felt that this was something she had to do, she also felt compelled to write a letter to her mother, to her brother and to her sister. I called her in Turkey on Sunday, June 22, 2008, to find out how she was and that she had made it safely there. She had a bit of a cold, but she said she was all right and that she thought she would come home earlier than expected and bring her mother with her. I was happy about that, because she would be there when I came down to Halifax to live. She had been getting blood transfusions and had to have permission from her doctor to travel. She did sound all right. On Friday morning, June 27, 2008, her son phoned me to tell me that she had died. My whole body went into shock. I refused to accept the news. I phoned her girls—one was at sea, as she was in the navy, but the other, to whom I spoke, was inconsolable. They went to Turkey to bring their mother's body back. Melani and I came down to attend the funeral, which had to be postponed until her pastor from her church in Calgary could come down to do the officiating. I have been upset since.

I finally retired after many lunches and dinners, and on September 2, 2008, Les and I drove down to Halifax in my car. This trip took four days, across country through the United States. It was enjoyable. Carl, my brother-in-law, flew down and drove back with Les.

During all these years, Deiter kept calling, and it was really nice to hear from him. I had Oona's children—Sonia, Klem, and Sara—over as often as possible. I made Thanksgiving dinner here and attended their birthdays. Jamie and Riley came to Nova Scotia for Christmas and that was a real treat for me. I had eight of us for Christmas dinner. I had my fruits on soak for my Christmas puddings and made several to be given away.

21
REMINISCING WITH DEITER

I would be remiss if I did not spend some time on the convictions that led me to write this book. I have explained to all my feelings of the love and confusion that consumed a big part of my life. I have also explained about the decisions I had to make in my youth when I felt that the love of my life had abandoned me. I married a most wonderful man who loved me dearly. He was not afraid to tell me and let me know just how much he loved me and just how precious I was to him. Above all, he gave me the space I needed to grow, to be myself, and to be who I am today, and I loved him dearly.

There was a confident and comfortable feeling in talking about and discussing anything with him. He taught me about life and love and gave me more than the comfort I needed to discuss and talk about very personal and private matters. It was just a very normal way of talking and doing things. Consequently, I have no hang-ups talking with comfort and asking questions, being serious, and being able to laugh and make fun of stupidity. Above all, he gave me love, and for over thirty years, this is how I lived. Being a good wife, a good homemaker, a good lover, and a good mother to our children were my priorities. When I was married to him, I loved him dearly, with all my heart, and now that he is no longer here, I truly miss him. After he passed away, I consoled myself with going back to school. As I said, I wanted no one else in my life, as I was not prepared to give things that anyone might have expected.

I was extremely happy when Deiter called, and our friendship continued. Early in our newfound friendship, he told me that he wanted more than friendship when I was only prepared for friendship; after all, he had a wife.

Over the years, we discussed so many things. He told me how he felt, he talked about his marriages, and he introduced me to one of his best "girl friends" on the phone. We argued, we made up, and we are still talking almost six years later. He has blamed me for our not being together and married. He told me that I took his heart when I left. He told me that he almost took his life. All this, I did not know. I just knew that when he did not write when he left, I felt abandoned. I felt that our friendship had ended, that he no longer cared, and that he had found someone else in the United States. Then, I saw his old girlfriend visiting with his parents. I was devastated. He owed me responses to sixteen or so unanswered letters that I wrote to him. After a multitude of tears, I stopped writing him. I needed to move on with my life. Then, I met the man who became my husband, for over thirty years. Les.

Deiter told me that if I had looked on the Internet, I would have found him. I did not know this, as I had no reason to try to find him, because I knew that he was married. So I began checking the Internet. I found him, all right, and I also found the name of his first wife and the blogs that she subscribed to. I decided to read them, and lo and behold, I found out so many things about his life. She had no sympathy about their lives and all that he supposedly did to her, and why she left him after thirty years of marriage. I really felt sorry for him, as he was a very private person and his life story unfolded on the Internet for the world to see. I was sorry for her also. I told him about it when he phoned, and he was so upset. I followed the blogs for a while, then got bored and felt intrusive, so I just stopped reading them.

Once, I really made him mad, and he did not talk to me for days. I tried to call him, but he would not answer his phone, and all I had wanted to say to him was, "I was really phoning to see how you were, because I felt our last conversation left us both depressed. You said you were depressed before. I did want to cheer you up, but I guess I messed up. I am very sorry. I am also sorry I made you mad." I had given him the reason why I did not marry him. Over these past six years, we have had many painful arguments and discussions, chief among them is the fact that I went away and married someone else. Most of the time, I have put my thoughts on paper because I got so upset and had difficulty talking about it to him.

Here is a letter from one of those arguments:

I have tried really hard to help you get over the stupidity of our youth—your lack of giving information and my not understanding. I was young and very naïve. I have since moved on, and I can talk about it without bitterness or malice. I do not want to talk about this again, although I feel that there is a lot of underlying animosity. I feel that there is a stalemate here, so we just have to leave it at that and perhaps just get on with our lives. You concentrate on your marriage, and I will just see what the future holds for me, as no matter what you think, I will never take any responsibility for what truly happened, and no matter how much you try to be a detective, you will always hear the same thing from me. You forced my life in the direction I had to take.

He was then having difficulty with his job, and he talked about that to me. He had minor medical problems, so we talked about that and about his changing schools. He was going through a very depressing period. We talked about that. I wanted to help him. I asked him if he talked to his wife. He said that he could not really talk to her. He never got a feeling of caring. She did not know how to help him. He went on to explain what a night at home was for him. He'd get home from his job as a high school counsellor. He'd lie on his couch and watch TV; then he'd get up, have something to eat, do some schoolwork on the computer, watch some more TV, and then go to bed. I knew he was lonely and unhappy in his relationship, but I also got a feeling of deep psychological issues, and I wanted to help.

We talked about possibilities and relationships, and he said that he knew that I wanted to have a relationship with him. I asked him if I was wrong in wanting a relationship. He said, "There is a possibility, perhaps soon." He did not know, however, how soon it would be. He would have to court me again. He wanted back the girl that he loved and who loved him; the girl who, when he kissed her, trembled in his arms. He had no doubt that she loved him, but he had not been in any position to marry her then. He also was not ready, so he could not. He had never, ever stopped loving me, he said, and I was the only person in this world who had ever seen the softer side of him. He did not want to tell me the things he knew I wanted to hear; he would, but it would not be fair to feed my insecurities. Even though we had parted, he did trust me and love me. He said I was a platelet and so was he, and when we were young, our platelets did not quite line up. And they had not yet quite lined up, but they would. He did not know when, but they would.

I responded, "I know one side of you, and it is this other side that shakes me, and perhaps I share some responsibility for it, and I am truly sorry. These are my own feelings on the last discussion we had. The things I said to you prior to that was to extract from you what you were thinking. The first thing you said was about me wanting to have a relationship with you. That may be so but in the sense of relationship, I was not and am not looking to you for a casual fling. I am not built that way. I would rather not have that, because I just can't, and I don't want to be called 'the other woman.' I was scared when you came here, because I felt that you were coming to put a closure to a love affair that had never been consummated. I knew I still loved you. It would have been easier if you had not said to me, 'So Marcey, where do we go from here?' That, to me, put life and hope in our friendship, and I really could not understand how you flipped from being loving to being callous and apparently uncaring. I, however, learned to live with it, as I was trying to see and understand who you have become after all these years.

"I did know the gentle and softer side of you, and that is who I continued to see and love. I have not changed; I am the same girl who, when you kissed her, trembled in your arms and who you had no doubt loved you. I have become more mature from life and experiences, but then, I am not sure about the life experiences, because I was protected from the harsh realities of life by a husband who loved me and cared for me—someone who I grew to love and who loved me in return. I know you were not thinking of marriage when we were young and going together; neither was I. I just wanted to be secure in the friendship we had, but perhaps I was also looking for tangible evidence in the things I hoped you would say and which you did not. This led to all my insecurities and heartache.

"I do feel honoured—actually, more than honoured—that I am the only person in this world who has seen the softer side of you, and as I said, that holds me to you. That side of you also makes me know who you truly are. It also helps me to understand you and where you are coming from. I look beyond your harshness and your thorns, because I know there is a wonderful, warm, loving, and very sensitive person there, and under all that, I admire your convictions and your rationale for who you have become. However, higher education allows us to reason. It does not make us who we always were.

"I don't want you to tell me anything that you don't want to tell me, in the event you may feed my insecurities. I am pretty secure within myself. It is the not knowing or having an idea of what you are thinking that makes me insecure. I like the truth and would rather hear you say, 'Marcey, this is not going to work,' or all the things you said on Tuesday regarding your not being in a position to give me the answers that you think I want. I already know this. I just want some comfort and some understanding that you at least care, and that we are and can remain friends. I don't like the cold. To me, this is a unique friendship. We were each other's first loves, and for me, it is hard to believe that you are really married, and I do tend to forget that one important item. I would like to tell you thanks for trusting me; that means a lot, as that is a major part of who I am. I am trustworthy. As for me, I have always trusted you. I just did not understand you in my youth and immaturity.

"You also talked about not knowing the motives, I believe, why I might love you or whatever. I have no motives, ulterior or otherwise, and as I said, if wanting to be with you and to take care of you and just love you are motives, then those are my motives. I have lived alone for many years and have managed to take care of myself. This is what I chose to do. I have no idea why you found me or why we are back in each other's lives. I have no answers except that my love for you engulfs me and that I know you love me also, and I guess the universe has something to do with it. I saw your spiritual side, because I believe in the alignment of the universe and the universal mind. There is a reason for our meeting again; there is a connection of the soul between us. There is something more between us, bigger than us, but as you said, our platelets are not quite aligned, and as you further said, 'But they will.' You don't know when, but they will.

"Because I have known and loved you for so long, I don't have a problem talking to you to let you know how I feel. I can be shy to a point, but when it comes to saying what I truly feel, I have learned to do this over the years, and I hope you don't have a problem with all that I have said. We have become so serious. It is time to laugh again. I need to laugh and bug you, as you have often bugged me."

As time went on, it appeared that we could not get past what broke us up in the beginning. I believed we had discussed this a million times, and it just seemed that we were going nowhere with this—there was just frustration and more frustration. I told him to grow up and get over it, as I had to. I was, however, still happy and secure in our newfound friendship, and he now called me very often, mostly in the mornings to wake me up. I loved that.

We continued talking over the years, and now, I decided to move to Halifax, Nova Scotia. In Halifax, our friendship became more intense.

He continued to call me every morning to wake me up and love me. We would speak for hours, and we also argued.

Here is another journal writing:

Having moved to Halifax, it seemed that our friendship became more intense. Here he is, living with his wife and talking seriously with me. Well, at least I think he was talking seriously. I came to the conclusion that any questionable thing that I have ever done in my life, I have done with him. He told me that he was working from three heads: one, the situation he was now in, being married; two, wanting to be with me; and three, wondering how long I would be willing to wait for him. Somehow, I felt that I just could not turn my back on him.

I asked him why he got married so soon after his divorce. He stated that he really had not wanted to get married, but she wanted to and kept bothering him to set a date. So he finally gave in, and he compromised because he was lonely after his divorce. I told him that he was a fool. He has stated that he wished he had waited. He said that if he'd known that I was alone, he would have come for me, and we would have been married by now. Somehow, I feel sorry for him. My heart does go out to him, actually, he has always made decisions that were detrimental, and that is why he lost me. On the other hand, I felt that if he had truly fought for me and not been so noncommittal, we might have been together, learning life together, and he would never have been divorced. But then, I was supposed to meet Les, and he truly pursued me, when Deiter abandoned me. Now, he has stated that our love was "puppy love," which was a real insult. Then he stated it became real when he phoned me in January 1965. I don't know what "puppy love" is, because I fell very deeply in love with him, and I have since stated that I would never love like that again. Another annoyance: he asked me to send him a Christmas pudding, which I did, and after keeping me "in the closet," so to speak, for five years, he showed his wife the package I sent. Her remark to that made me angry; he told me she'd asked him if he got that from "his old flame." I am not his old flame. I have never been his flame, and that made me extremely mad, and I voiced my disapproval to that statement.

Deiter has not always been honest with his information. He has everyone believing that I was the bad one in our friendship, and that I was the one that left him when he went to university to make a life for "us." Lord knows just how many people there hate me that I don't even know. I moved on with my life, because I wrote him sixteen letters, and he never responded. I thought he was my boyfriend, but I soon realized I was wrong—he did not care, so I thought I had better heal my broken heart, as I felt that he had found someone else in the States, an American girl. He has also not been truthful when he tells everyone that I was the one who found him on the Internet and phoned him after thirty-eight years. He was the one that found me and phoned me. On December 27, 2003, he rekindled this love affair, and then came to see me and has constantly called me. I did ask about him, but I would have never phoned him, because I thought he was married to his first wife.

I wish I was not so trusting, because I really feel so used. I am up against a wife, an ex-wife, and a special "girl friend." Then, here I am. I have prayed to God so many times, saying that if this is to be, please let it be; if not, then please remove this from me. It has been over five years, and he is still here. This Christmas 2008 and New Year's 2009 have been soul-searching times for me. Should I go? It is a hard decision, but maybe I should. Should I stay? Why? What for? I prefer truth and honesty. He also needs to remember that I had been married for over thirty years.

22
ANALYZING DEITER, THEN AND NOW

I put my thoughts on paper quite a bit, but that is where it stays. I wrote two poems; I wrote about him, then and now:

THIS MAN
THEN:
    My first attraction was his sense of humour. Looking deeper, his eyes were deep and very warm. There was always a subtle, sneaky smile on his lips, and they were very inviting. His heart was beautiful, warm, and very caring. His lanky body oozed a sexual attraction that made my body shake when he put his arms around me and held me and as he also shook. It appeared that we could not get enough of each other; we were "kids." Then he made me mad; I made him mad. I don't think all the icebergs in the Arctic could be as cold as I felt due to the deep freeze I experienced in the months before he left for university. I persevered. I did everything. I tried to find out why. I never did. I persevered some more and wrote every week, once I got his address. By then, I was concerned. This love affair was one of the past, but I held it together on my end; then I gave up the futile battle. "Marcey, you cannot make someone love you if they don't and don't want to." My self-esteem was at an all-time low.
    Ten months of uncertainty—come on, girl, move on with your life. Then he phoned, and although he did not tell me that he loved me, he asked me, and I said yes, and that was the truth. I questioned and wondered why he phoned me. Did someone there give him the "old heave-ho" so he came running back? I was suspicious. Or did someone from the island tell him

that I had begun to see someone else? It was the latter, I was convinced. I did not believe the sudden resurgence in affection, when I considered the way in which he treated me all those months before, and before he left, and the way in which he left the island, and all my sixteen or more unanswered letters. I really had to harden my heart, as there were emotional remnants of a love that shook my heart, my soul, and my entire being. Then our letters crossed. His was finally full of all that I wanted to hear, and mine, not good at all, since he had not written or responded to any of my letters for months, I did not know he was going to write. I had wanted to write him one more letter, in my time, to tell him that I was engaged to be married, but with help, the letter I wrote was cut-and-dried and so much unlike me. Six months later (not the four years he had said), he came home. The man I saw was not the man that left me on my veranda the previous year. He was quiet, very subdued, and every emotion we felt for each other in the beginning of our friendship could hardly be contained, and I knew I still loved him.

NOW:

After thirty-eight years of separation, he found me and called me. I am now a widow, and have been for eight years. He was divorced in 1999 and has been remarried since 2002. He phoned me on December 27, 2003. That emotional bond we both shared all those many years ago is still very strong, but he has a wife. In almost six years of contact, I have seen him twice. I have found him to be a man of conflicting thoughts, very intelligent, and when I asked him in the beginning, "Deiter, what are we going to do about this?" He said, "It is going to be messy." That alone gave me hope to continue talking to him. One minute, he tells me that he loves me; the next minute, it is as if he never said it. He asked me to wait for him; then the next minute, he states he can't ask me, that it will be up to me. One minute, he is going to come to see me; the next minute, he does not know how and when he can get away. One minute, he is very upset with his wife; the next minute, she is beautiful. One minute, I have far exceeded the beauty of anyone he has known, meaning his two wives. The first wife, the mother of his children, divorced him after over thirty years of marriage. The second wife wanted him to marry her, so he did. He has stated the regrets in his life and sometimes holds me responsible for the choices he has had to make. He states that he wants to be with me, but he does nothing about it. I am not excited at the predicament in which I find myself, but I feel that I cannot turn my back on this man. His mother, in a dream, told me that he needed a lot of love and that I must give him that love, which won't be hard to do. There are times I would just like to run away and hide so I cannot be found, but for whatever the reason, I just don't seem to be able to.

I have lived a very uncomplicated life with my husband, whom I loved dearly, and our three children. That was all I needed. When he died, I was not interested in having another relationship, as I felt I was fortunate once to find and marry a man who truly loved me and who gave me the space to be me and to grow into who I am today. Thank God for that, because with that knowledge, it would appear that I can deal with what is now thrown at me—conflict, indecisions, self-esteem issues—and I believe I can hold any conversation that is thrown at me because of the openness of my life, my heart, and of the self that I shared with my husband. It is his conflicting statements and thoughts of a mind and soul that is in conflict with self—uncertainty, unhappiness, depression. How can I help? Leave or stay? But he has a wife who should be more watchful. Although I understand this man a lot more than I did when I was young, there is a little way further in understanding to go. Just by talking to him, I immediately know when he is sick; I know when he is upset; I know when he feels depressed; I know when he feels love for me; I also know when he tries to hide things that are bothering him. I know when he wants to talk and when he does not want to talk. I feel his tormented heart, I know he wants to be with me, and I know he is torn, and on top of all that his eyes are deep and sad and still very warm. His lips are still very inviting, and his heart is still beautiful, warm, and very caring, and I love him now, more that ever, if that can be possible.

I do not know where all this will lead. If he loves his wife, and if he is happy, then I will just disappear.

23
VISIT TO ATLANTA AND DISAGREEMENT

The year 2009 started off well, with lots of snow and rain. My birthday was good. Deiter phoned me and serenaded me as I opened my eyes. I went for lunch and then dinner. My children all phoned. Leslie sent me a box of chai tea in several flavours, and Melani sent me a blank book in which to record my poems and my thoughts. On February 2, 2009, I would be leaving for Newark, New Jersey, to spend ten days with my brother in Jackson. From there, I would go to Toronto to spend twelve days with Zickle and her family. I was due back home on February 24, 2009. I knew that Deiter would call me on my cell every day that I was away.

I believe I have poured my soul into this book. Some things I have repeated, but I needed to put them in the context of what I was trying to explain. I still loved this man. He wanted me to come to Atlanta, and although I had thought of it, my values would be compromised. He needed to make a decision regarding our lives if he wanted to be with me; then he should come here. He needed peace, safety, and happiness. Although it was nice to hear from him, and although my heart skipped several beats and the old feelings resurfaced—that I was the love of his life; that he had been trying to find me all these years—it really was a lot to process in that short space of time. Although we had so much to catch up on, in the back of my head there was uncertainty, and it appeared as if history was repeating itself. Deiter, like it was then, was with Kitty, now he was married, and I, like is was before, was unattached and now, I am still unattached I know what I would have liked to have happen, but it was not my decision. I just knew that I wanted no more heartache. As for me, he would never get heartache because of me. A platonic friendship was not what I wanted from him. I didn't know what he wanted from me. I just knew I didn't want to be hurt, and I supposed a talking friendship was better than no friendship for another thirty-eight years. But then, did I really want this?

Well, he kept asking me to come to Atlanta by saying, "I know you are coming. I just don't know when." I searched within myself for some sign, both inward and outward, of whether I should go. I did get my tickets to travel and booked myself into a hotel, as I did not want to stay at his house. Then he got pneumonia and was confined for several weeks, and I felt that was a sign. I cancelled everything. He asked me again at the end of his confinement. I went through the same process, and this time, it just seemed as though everything went smoothly. I had not seen him for almost five years.

He met me at the airport—a sight for sore eyes. I was so happy to see him, and seeing his home and the sights of Atlanta with him was enjoyable. Our love was exciting, and we truly loved each other. I was content in just being with him. This felt so natural.

I congratulated him on his effort in building his home. I loved his gardens; they were well cared for and beautiful. I could see where he put all his love. We went shopping for more plants. His wife was away somewhere on a course. I did not know this before I arrived. In the evenings, we went back to the hotel. I kept searching for tangible evidence that he was giving me his undivided attention, but perhaps I was looking too hard. I felt that he might have been a little absent. We did do a lot of talking, and he loved me, but I kept searching for his soul. There were times when I thought I had found it, but at others, there appeared to be something missing. He appeared to be so unhappy and sometimes deep in thought. Yet I knew he loved me. It was now time for me to go back to Canada, and we kissed each other so lovingly. I can still remember his standing at the airport until I was out of sight; I have often remembered this. I was as happy as I could be, yet I had mixed feelings. I knew that I loved him, but I wanted more.

The year 2009 did not end so well. Deiter and I had a fuss after his birthday in November, and we did not talk for weeks. I went to Calgary for Christmas to be with my children. When I got home in January, I relented and called him. We made up and talked at length. I had phoned Frederick on Christmas to wish him a Merry Christmas, and he told me that he had been in the hospital and that he had had open-heart surgery. This scared me, so I phoned Cara to tell her. Before I left for Calgary, I checked on

Frederick and told him that I would call him again when I got home. He had moved from his house, so I could not call, as I did not have his new phone number. I got it from Cara, as Deiter had phoned her to give her the number. I called Frederick the following morning to see how he was, and I continued to do so. By this time, Deiter and I were talking regularly again. He kept phoning me every morning, sometimes twice per day.

The last time I phoned Frederick was the week before Easter, and he told me that he had taken a turn in his recuperation and that he was not so well. I encouraged him to go to the hospital, but he said he did not want to go. Deiter phoned, and I told him what Frederick had said and that I felt really scared.

Deiter phoned me on April 6 to tell me that Frederick had passed away. I was in shock. I phoned Karen, his wife, right away. I prepared to go to his funeral on April 10, so I caught a flight out on the ninth and stayed with Cara. She told me that Deiter had phoned her and told her to tell me that he was bringing his wife and that he did not want to be stressed out. I was furious, because I did not know to what or to whom his comment referred.

The funeral was so sad. I met Karen for the first time, although I had talked to her on the phone several times. I liked her, and this connection was instantaneous. I met Deiter's wife. I was a little uncomfortable; he was also uncomfortable, or so it appeared. I watched the dynamics between them, and I am not too sure if I understand their relationship. I saw no expressions of love there. We all went over to Karen's house after the funeral, and Deiter spent a lot of time sitting and talking with us, while his wife sat at a table with other friends. She never came over to talk to us. Considering that he had introduced us to her, she was not very warm. Well, he told the people we were talking to that I was the love of his life. This made me mad. He left to return to his sister's house, where they were staying. I went back to Cara's, and then on Sunday, I went to spend a few days with my cousin.

Deiter phoned me there on Monday and Tuesday mornings. I left on Wednesday to get back to Halifax. He phoned me on Thursday morning to see if I got home okay. He continued to call me every day. On the following Monday, we talked. Then on Tuesday when he phoned, we were talking and laughing as we bugged each other. I don't know what I said, but something I said drove him off the deep end, and he was really mad at me, and I could not understand why. I believe he must have had an argument with his wife, and I was now in the line of fire. I said to him, "Do not get upset with me, I don't even know what I said." I then asked him if he was going to spend the rest of his life with his wife; he said he did not know. I asked him if he planned to spend the rest of his life with me. He said he did not know, and that he never plans anything, and that he did not know that he would have been divorced. I asked him if he loved me, and he said yes. I asked him if he was coming to Nova Scotia, and he said that he would like to come, but he did not know when he could.

He brought up again that I'd left him and married someone else. I said, "Then why did you not make a commitment? I would have married you." He said that he had not wanted to. That was a first for me; he had never said that before. I then said, "Then why did you call me after you were in your new marriage for one year?" He said he was sorry that he had—another first. He was really miserable and was really telling me off. I told him that I could not argue with him, and that I was not a confrontational person, and that I was tired of all this. I told him that I felt I was being held hostage. He wanted to know by whom. I asked him just who did he think I was. He said, "You are just a friend." He was really mean, and I accused him of being "hard." I was upset, so I told him that he should let me go, as I did not want this anymore. He asked me if I did not want him to call me anymore. I told him it was up to him whether he wanted to or not. He said, "That is not what I asked you." I then said, "That might be a good idea." I told him that he should just let me go so that I could live my life, as I was hurting, and to this he said that he knew that. I said that I was tired of all this and did not want this anymore, and that I had been here before, and that I learned to handle it all, and that I could do it again. I suggested that he pay attention to his wife and his marriage.

I further reminded him that he'd asked me to come to Atlanta. I was glad to see him and to spend time with him, but ever since I came back, in June of last year, something was amiss. I would have been happy with a few kisses, some hugs and some cuddles—nothing more. I stated that I wanted no favours from him. I was no fool; I knew what love was—I'd had one man to whom I had been married for over thirty years, and now him. Love to me is meaningful. I said, "I sure felt nothing from you; therefore, I could do nothing myself. I said, "Just let me be. Let me get on with my life." I reminded him of all the things he said to me over the past almost seven years—how he loved me and that he wanted to marry me and to spend the rest of his life with me but he had a predicament.. I told him good-bye. I heard him say good-bye quietly, and then I hung up the phone. I was livid. I had only ever been livid once before in my life, and that was with my husband over a game of checkers. This was more serious and I hoped he was as hurt as I was.

I did not hear from Deiter after that. I still loved this man, but I would not call him. He did have a wife.

Well, Deiter did call me again, and it was good to hear from him. We talked about the quarrel we had, and made amends with each other. He continued to call daily, sometimes twice daily. I knew he had a wedding anniversary in August, so I asked him what did he do to celebrate this occasion. He told me that he took his wife out to dinner and then dancing. I was a little upset at his response. I asked him how many years had he been married, and he said 9 years. I was a little more upset again at his response, as he had been phoning me for 7 of those 9 years.

I said to him that he appeared to be comfortable in his marriage, therefore what did he want from me, and where was he going in terms of telling me that he loved me? Was he going to stay in his marriage, or was he going to be with me?

I reminded him of all the things he said to me. I then asked him what did I mean to him. He said I was his friend, so I said to him that I did not kiss my friends, neither did I make love with my friends.

Once again he repeated that he did not know what was going to happen because he did not know that he would have been divorced from his first wife. Again he brought up the fact that we would not be having this conversation if I had not married Les. He further stated that I probably thought he was a bad person, that I thought he lies, and that I thought he used me. To this, I neither agreed or disagreed.

He also said that he knew I would never believe that he loved me unless he was standing there in front of me telling me that he loved me. I agreed. He did not like this inquisition, as I was the one asking all the questions. He wanted me to stop as he had to go, so I accused him of trying to run away as he always did. I wanted some answers, as I wanted to know in what direction my life was headed. I finally got some answers, and now, I had to deal with all that I had heard. I had long since admitted that we both made mistakes for two people who are so much in love with each other. I will take responsibility for not being more trusting, for not waiting to hear from him, and for marrying someone else, but, I was humiliated, I was upset, and above all I felt that he no longer loved me, and that I would never see him again. I will say that his mistake was not communicating his true feelings for me before he left, not corresponding while he was away, and not responding to any of the sixteen letters I wrote to him, one every week. I have often stated to him that his lack of not doing what he should have done, has resulted in any and all the decisions that I have had make in my life.

I once again retreated within myself, and with serious thinking, I concluded that this friendship was really going nowhere, and I had to make some decisions. I would never call him or respond to any of his calls again.

Here, I now had to see where my strengths and weaknesses lie, to try to get through this period in my life. I searched my soul to find where they lie, and why was it so difficult to ask the questions that I needed to ask Deiter from so many years ago. I found that my strengths are the love for people and being true to those I love, because in turn, they give me my strength. My weaknesses are not taking care of my well being as I should and not being able to say "no" and really mean it. I have difficulty saying things that will hurt another human being. I am long- suffering, and will absorb a lot of pain and hurt as I have done over these past 7 years. Well, I have now come to my breaking point, and I don't want to hurt anymore.

24
HOPE, DEEP IN THOUGHT

Then, one morning in May, my doorbell rang. I slowly got up, put my housecoat on, and went to answer the call. As I opened the door, there before me was a very tall man with graying hair and penetrating but very gentle eyes. He was carrying a suitcase, and he asked me, "Will you take me in forever?" I almost collapsed, as my legs went weak. Without a response to his question, I flew into his arms and did not give him an opportunity to say another word. I just kissed him. "Yes, oh, yes, and forever!" I said. We clung to each other, wishing that forty-five years of pain and hurt would melt away. I pulled him inside and closed the door .Then, for hours, we loved, we talked, and we loved, we talked about past, present and a future together as we tried to get through the forty-five years we had been apart. In my youth, I did not understand, and instead of waiting, I ran away, because I felt he no longer cared. In maturity, we both suffered as we waited over seven years—or perhaps forty-five years—to finally be together again. I felt my aching heart come to life as it fluttered with happiness and blessings from my guardian angels, who had worked so hard on our behalf.

I have now finally come full circle, and we are never going to let go of each other ever again. This is my ultimate wish and prayer.

This ending was written two years ago, and today, I question myself once again, what have I learned from all this turmoil and heartache? I learned that I am a very strong person, I am comfortable being myself, and have realized that I don't need anyone to make me whole. I need to be whole first. I have done great work for others as a social worker. I should turn inwards to look at and take care of myself first, or I cannot help anyone. I should have discerned the manipulation and not been so trusting. I should have questioned thoroughly the sincerity of this approach, yet, I still love this man, and I always will.

My greatest lesson is that everyone is not alike, and I don't ever want to lose the love and trust that I have for people, as my training tells me, that people are not bad, it is only their actions that are considered questionable or bad.

25

BACK IN THE SHADOWS

At the end of my last chapter, I wrote what I had hoped would have happened and soliloquized about what I would do, but was not truly convinced that I could carry through with my thoughts. I was determined however never to take any more calls from Deiter, after all he had a wife. I, however, went back in time to December of 2003 when Deiter first phoned me after 38 years. I also recalled the first letter he sent me, dated January 12, 2004.

> "Dear Marcey,
>   That term seems so inadequate. But just to say "Marcey" and know that my shining star is still bright and warm and just "Marcey." It sounds so good and feels so safe and clean and cozy. You will never know how much I've missed you………
>
> With Love
> Deiter.

He sent me a hand drawn Valentine's Card, including a gift.
I responded to his Valentine's greeting with a Card and a letter from my heart, dated February 7, 2004.

> "Dearest Love,
>   Here I go again, putting pen to paper to try to express what I find difficult to verbalize, and here I thought I was this person who was so mature and open…..I am just so happy to be able to

talk to you, to hear your voice and feel your love coming at me through the telephone lines. It is as if we were back 39 years (to be exact) that had separated us, and you called, and I would take the phone into the hallway by my bedroom, sat on the floor for long periods of time, just talking to you. You have no idea how I have missed you, and how I have missed talking to you, and with all your subtle rudeness.

I would like to know the powers that be that magically struck my heart that rendered me helpless and totally attracted to you. Perhaps unknown to both of us there was a spark, because I loved your sense of humour, as you could always make me laugh, and you always teased me to see me blush, then Mr. Acker Bilk came along and cast his spell. This attraction became bigger than me, and I believe you felt the same way because this developed into passionate love that stayed with me, but I had to deny this because of forces unknown and that I did not understand, and broken as I was, I did turn to someone else, because I had lost you, at least I thought I had.

I have no idea why two souls, two hearts as passionate and in love as ours must suffer so, and I know you have because you told me so. I also know I have because I told you so. Is this our destiny? Loving each other as much as we do and for so long, and never getting together because our timing is not right, or must we steal time together? I guess I would rather do that than wait another 39 years just to say "my love" to you.

I have never been able to understand what it was, or what it still is that holds us together. I know it is love and passion and that other something else that is bigger than us, because of the six of us that were friends together, it appears that we are the only ones that have had that eternal love for each other albeit, perhaps battered and bruised, but it is still there, because I love you Deiter Chabot, I always have, and I always will.

Happy Valentine's My Love
As Always"

Well, Deiter and I could not resist not being able to talk to each other, at least, Deiter, it appeared could not keep the silence between us, so he would be the one that always phoned, and I was always glad to hear from him every day. I knew him so well; I knew he would never apologize even knowing that he was the one that said the things that were hurtful. I learned to deal with it, so I followed suit, and got back at him at a later date. I just assumed that he was sorry, because he was always the one that called again, because I knew he missed talking to me; actually, I missed him too.

He would phone Karen, perhaps to see if I ever wanted to talk to him again. She would tell me just how terrible he was feeling.

He would tell her "Marcey fired me."

She would tell him that people who love each other don't "fire each other."

He went on to tell her – "I love that girl so much, she has brought such joy to my life, and she has filled the gap in my life. I know she is frustrated and so she has dumped me."

He stated to her that he wanted to leave his current situation.

Karen stated that she said "Your love for Marcey is far too deep not to have any communication." She asked him if his wife knew about me. He stated "she knows, about Marcey, because I told her – darn right I told her – she had to know."

He told her that for years he had been searching for me, he even paid a Private Detective to find me. He did find me, but I was still married, so he stopped. He was just so happy that I was still alive. He also told her that if he had known that I was alone later, he would have never married his current wife, and that he and I would now be married, and we would be together for the rest of our lives, and t hat he would be so happy for the rest of his life.

He phoned me after his conversation with Karen.

I would at a later date ask him why did he not try to find me before he married again, He told me that he could not afford to pay another Private Investigator. I then asked him, why did he not he use the same method he used now, then, to find me. Getting Cara's phone number, then, phoning Cara to get my phone number. He was mad at himself and could not really answer.

26
MORE LOSS AND HEALTH PROBLEMS

Although I had spent time with Cara, I did not detect that she was very ill. This I found out in September of 2010, the same year Frederick died.

It was discovered that she was in the final stages of breast cancer, which had spread throughout her body and into her bones. I was devastated. So both Karen and I prayed seriously for her recovery.

I made a second trip to Florida in 2010 to visit with Cara, who was now bedridden and was being cared for at home. She was comatose, but responded to me when she heard my voice. I could not contain my tears, Two days later; she was no longer with us.

My heart was so sad. I phoned Deiter and Donald to tell them she had passed.

That was two of my very best friends in one year. One in April and the other in November. I could not stay in Florida for Cara's funeral, as due to the American Thanksgiving, they could not have it until sometime in December.

2011 rolled around, Deiter continued to call every morning to wake me. We would talk for hours, he would sing to me, and there was a lot of laughter. We really loved each other and I could hear and feel his frustration as he really wanted to be with me. He was also very glad that Les had taken care of me.

Deiter had not been feeling well for sometime, headaches, back problems, tiredness and colds. His doctor advised that he should have his kidneys checked, so he went to the hospital to have a biopsy done on one of his kidneys. In the process, they felt it necessary to take a further biopsy on his lymph nodes.

I had phoned him in the hospital to see how he was. He went home the next day. I went to Calgary to be with my daughter Melani. Deiter phoned me in Calgary to tell me that his kidney was fine, but his lymph nodes were not, and Lymphoma was diagnosed.

Not knowing anything about Lymphoma, I panicked and consulted family members and friends in the Medical profession who put my mind at ease, letting me know that immediate death was not on the agenda, and that persons with that cancer, could live with it for a long time.

Deiter's health was a concern, but I did not let him know how I worried. There were times when he was really down, but being the avid gardener that he was, he worked a lot outside. I was, however, concerned about his eating habits, and of course, the amount of energy he expended to move rocks, to get loads of mulch, to volunteer at his Master Gardener organization, to design, and work on gardens for his friends, to make furniture for his children, to baby-sit his grandchildren, and to cook Jamaican food for friends and family and the multitude of other things he did. He called me everyday, sometimes twice. Most times, the second call was when he would say "Babes, I need to have a rest, just stay with me for a bit. I would, then hang up the phone when I heard his quiet snore as he fell asleep. He was so tired.

Deiter's calls became more intense, we talked about so many things, he wanted to go "home," and home was Jamaica. I felt the same, so we talked a lot about Jamaica. He talked about his love for me, and I would say "I don't know why I love you," and he would say "let me count the ways," then he would repeat every negative name I called him, then I would be reduced to stitches of laughter. He also said silly things to me when he knew I was mad at him. He always accomplished what he set out to do, reduce me to laughter, and my being upset would be gone with the wind.

I finally came to the conclusion that if he had a fuss at home with his wife, he would be miserable with me. I learned that. He told me that he would love to win the lottery. I asked him what would he do with his winnings, he said he would pay out his wife, then go home and build a home on his farm for the both of us. I also bought tickets on the lottery here, so I asked him if he knew why I bought tickets, and he said "so you can share it with me." He was right.

I now began to understand why Deiter asked me if I wanted him to divorce his wife. He was frustrated, he felt trapped and he was checking to see if I really loved him, or was I going to be there for him if he did leave. I had never asked him to leave his wife.

He asked me so many questions about my life with Les; it was as if he was trying to see what our life would be when we got together. One of the things he told me was that Carlene had asked him if he knew me any better after all the years we had been talking to each other. He said he told her that he knew the very core of me.

So, I asked him "if you do, then what have you discovered about my core?" He said "Marcey, you are a good woman, a really good woman." I then retorted with a "thanks" and further said, "I am just a girly girl."

He told me he loved who I was, he loved the shape of my body, and he further said that he has never loved anyone as he had loved me. I cried.

He made me very nervous with things he said. He once told me that he was so tired, he felt his skin sliding off from his bones. That frightened me, so I gave him trouble, as I felt he needed some rest. He talked about his mother, he said, she was the only person who would really know what was wrong with him without him having to tell her anything. He told me that he wanted to die before me, so I asked him why, and he said, "I could not live knowing that you were not here." He told me that he wanted to go home to Jamaica alone, he did not want his wife with him, he just wanted to be alone, and in the next breath, he asked me if I would meet him there, and how soon would I be able to get away, as he was going to work on how he could get away. I told him that he was so controlled, how could he do that. I did know, however, that I would do everything that I could to meet him there. He sounded so very sad and so trapped.

He further told me that he did not think he had five more years to live. That really scared me again, so I told him he should not talk like that, he was scaring me, and that only God knew that. I, however, did not forget his omen. I cried again.

27
ALONE AGAIN

On May 24th, 2012, he called me, and we spoke to each other for almost two hours. He said he had just finished varnishing the floor in his family room. He said he had to go as he had an appointment to design a garden for a couple, and he still had to shave and shower.

I did not want to let him go, especially when he told me just how tired he was. We talked a lot, he sang to me, we laughed a lot, we loved each other, and I will always remember what he told me. "Marcey, I just want to sit here and do nothing, just do nothing, you and I, we would just sit here and do nothing, and we would have so much fun, just doing nothing, we would be so happy, then we could go over to the swing, we could swing and just do nothing." I thought that would be a good idea as I would have loved just doing "nothing" with him, that was all I ever wanted.

Again he said he had to go, so I said "OK, good luck and be careful." He said he would call me if he got home early. I was the one that said "OK, I'll let you be." He was very quiet when he said 'ÒK' as though he did not want to get off the phone. I did hang up, but was very puzzled at his quietness, and I wondered about that, and I thought of calling back, but I knew he was busy. I went off and made some muffins, as I had told him that that was what I was about to do.

Karen called me later that evening to tell me of the accident and that Deiter was 'no longer with us. My mind and my body went into shock. It was less than an hour that I had last talked to him that the accident happened. My mind could not, and refused to comprehend. Once again, and as I felt when he was leaving to go to University those many years ago,

I felt as though a magnet had taken all my life and energy from me, I felt naked, and very, very alone.

As Deiter had always said to me; "When I die, I want you to come to my funeral." I said to him "how could I." He had so many people from his past and his present that would be there. He said, "Marcey, you will be the number one person there, above everyone else."

I did go to Atlanta to attend his funeral, and I stayed with Carlene from May 30 to June 2, 2012. I met all his children and got acquainted again with his brothers and sister that I knew when Deiter and I were young and going out together in Jamaica, so many years ago. We hugged and remembered each other. A picture I had given Deiter many years ago, and which he carried in his wallet, was returned to me by his wife, as she said `Marcey, I have something for you that Deiter would like you to have.` I went over to his home, and sat on the same chair that he was sitting on when he last spoke to me. I did a lot of crying, and even more when I boarded the aircraft to return home.

There are no more words to express the sense of loss I feel, so I decided to write a letter to him which expresses our love and every sentiment we have ever felt and shared.

I also thought of the painful life he must have had, losing his four year old sister at a young age, losing his four year old brother in his early teenage years, losing his father, Then his mother and losing me, the love of his life as he so often told me. So much pain in the life of one human, and I have lived every one of these losses with him.

Deiter was a man of many personalities, he was brilliant, very versatile, very kind and had so much love and empathy for so many, especially the students he taught and counselled, but he could still compartmentalize the things that had the most meaning in his life, and that was his children and his love for me, and the love we shared.

28
A LETTER TO DEITER

My Dearest Love,

Everything is at a "standstill." I just can't seem to be able to get beyond that Atlanta Highway that took you from me. I see your tired body succumb to illness, as you drive. I see your car weaving across the highway. I see your car swerving on the highway. I see your lifeless body slumped over the steering wheel of your car. I see your car roll over and your lifeless body was crushed. Then I looked at my telephone to see that you had called me at 11.35AM Nova Scotia time, which was 10.35AM Atlanta time. The day was Thursday May 24, 2012. We had talked until 11.40AM Atlanta time.

You had just completed staining your floors in your family room which took you several days, and you said you did it without any help. You had been up at 6.00AM you said to go to the store to get more varnish. You had just completed the job, and we talked for over an hour. You were going to shave and shower because you told me that you had a 1.00PM appointment with clients who were interested in having you design a garden for them.

Approximately, and less than an hour after we hung up our phones, you were gone, taking that other journey to heaven, and I was not there to be with you. Oh God, how I miss you!!!

Our last telephone conversation was one of happiness and joy, you sang to me, you so wanted to be with me, you wanted us to be together and so you said:

"Marcey, I just want to sit here and just do nothing with you, just do nothing. Just to be with you. We would have so much fun and we would be so happy."

I told you how much I loved you. I told you the reasons why I did, and among the reasons were your rudeness and your sense of humour, your beautiful heart and your "sexy self." You asked me if I thought you were sexy, I affirmatively responded, and then we went into stitches of laughter at your rude comment. That was the first time I had ever told you that you were sexy. How I loved to hear you laugh!! You also told me that you knew the very core of me, so I asked if you did, what did you discover about my core. You said:

"You are such a good woman. I love you, I love everything about you, I love your shape, and I love who you are."

I retorted with a thanks, and went on to say, I am just a "girly girl" and that is just who I am.

At the end of our conversation, I told you that I had better "let you go" so you could shave and shower. I wished you good luck and "take care." I was a bit puzzled after I hung up the phone, as you did not sound your cheerful self, it was as if you did not want me to get off the phone. That bothered me all afternoon, but you said you would call me later if you got back home early.

I cannot get past the phone call late at night to tell me of your accident, and that you were no longer here with us. My body experienced such shock, one that I cannot get over the devastation I felt, which I still have not accepted.

These last few years were wonderful, you called me almost every day and when you did not, I gave you trouble for not calling. We talked every morning, and sometimes during the afternoons and at night when you were alone. I felt I knew your plans, but you could not verbalize them to me, you told me that I had no patience, imagine, I agreed!!

You told me about redoing the floors in your family room etc. You told me you did not really want to do them, how tired you were. I asked if you had any help, you said "no." I offered to help you. You said your back was sore, I asked if you got a massage, you said "no." I offered to do that. I was so angry because I felt that you needed to be taken care of.

I felt your love as I imagined you lying beside me every morning as we talked on the phone. I cracked up with laughter at your rudeness. You could always make me laugh. Then we both cracked up at the names I called you, especially when I told you that I was going to tell your mother the rude things you told me. I often asked you "where did your mother find you, I believe she found you under a rock." I also said that I did not know why I loved you, and you would say "let me count the ways, idiot, jackass, stupid, jerk," and more. With this, you made me laugh so much as I retorted with the same adjectives again, making you laugh. We just could not stop giggling. Then when you made me mad, you always said something funny in the midst of everything, which made me crack up with laughter. I so loved those times. I believe we both made each other happy, although at times, I felt that you were afraid to be happy.

We talked about love, you told me that you did not know what love was after you lost me. You said you had it once, all the fuzzy feelings, the purity of it, and then the pain you suffered after you thought it was gone. You told me that I was the one that taught you what that love was, that you have never loved anyone as you have loved me. That you gave me every ounce of your love, and that you could never take it back. Kissing each other was the extent of our love as we dared not go any farther, we were young, and we did not know anything beyond that.

I remember you telling me that you wished you were a selfish person, just doing what you really wanted and not caring who got hurt. You always tried to speak in riddles, sometimes I deciphered them, but at times, I overanalysed everything, as you would tell me. Oh, how I should have encouraged you, but, that was not you, neither was that me.

I kept your company on the phone when you were tired and you would fall asleep. I would hear your quiet snore. I kept your company when you were alone. I kept your company, told you how and cooked Jamaican dishes with you. I listened to you and tried to cheer you up when you were upset. You told me you trusted me with your life, and I did you with mine. We told each other so many secrets about ourselves, and as you would call yourself "just plain old Simple Simon," but I knew just how smart and intelligent you were. I knew when you were in a good mood, I knew when you were in a bad mood and not happy about a situation. I knew your soul as you knew mine. You tried my patience until I got so very mad, then you would call again, and we would be in love again.

Your life was truly not your own. All around you wanted a part, if not all of it. You were truly controlled by all, and you appeared not to be able to do anything about it. I felt your sadness.

I helped you tend your beautiful gardens and walked your property with you. I went to the mailbox with you, all this on the phone. Then I came to see you and literally did the same. I saw you tend your plants, and saw the love you gave to them, and you showed me just how you did your gardening. I saw where you put your love, this I know, because I experienced the same. I sat on your swing under your pergola and listened to your waterfall, as I watched your fishes swimming around. I cooked for you at your home, and watched you eat.

At your house, I also watched you sleep on your couch and listened to your quiet snore, before I also fell asleep. I felt your arms around me when we were younger, they were the best, and I felt safe. I felt your lips on mine, and they ignited such a force throughout my body, that was my first experience and introduction to falling in love. We felt the same, and an eternal bond was formed. I felt your arms and your lips again, and once again the flames were ignited with more force.

What have I learned, that love, our love is eternal. I know I will never be the same without you. I have been loved and I have loved two incredible men, in very different ways. You were my first love and the love of my life. We were married spiritually, in this life and so shall this remain.

The pureness of your heart is what I loved, your love of people, especially for the less fortunate. The special friendships you formed especially with Karen and Carlene, who are special blessings to me at this time. You fought for justice, whether it was the popular thing to do or not. Your friends were very important to you. Family and home had a priority in your life, if only it would have been returned as freely as you gave. Happiness, somehow eluded you as you lost the most important people in your life, your parents. We may have displaced each other for a while, but we never really lost each other, because I knew deep in my heart that we would see each other again.

Funny how life really is, you knew what you wanted, but you

did not know how to get it. I knew what I wanted and left it open, vulnerable and very available for you. You just did not know how to reason and make the right decisions you really wanted to make. As for me, I really wanted you, but I did not know either, how to do the persistent thing because of both our upbringings, boys were the ones that did the chasing, and girls waited until they were told what step was next. You felt you had nothing to offer me, how silly, I did not want material things from you, all I wanted was you. You, and more of you. I had not even thought of marriage, just security in a loving friendship.

When you left for University, I was dying slowly from all the emotions you opened up in me and taught me, I could not hide them, and I tried so hard to put that fire out as your actions dictated otherwise. Decisions for you in times of crisis were not an asset for you. Decisions for me were things I could make, whether they were for the best or not, as once I made them, I stuck with them because I was committed.

I waited on you to tell me what you had decided, but you were silent. I knew what you wanted, but I could do nothing until you told me. Once again, I did not want material things from you, I just wanted you. I have always told you, that the things you did not say and the decision that you did not make, because you had nothing to offer me, was a direct result of the decision I ultimately made. Thank God that the decision I made was a good one, as for over thirty years, I was loved and taken care of by a good man, until God called him home, and before he left, he sent me back to you.

Then you called me after thirty eight years, and immediately the love I had always had for you, was evident. I was so happy and scared at the same time, I did not know what to expect. I knew you still loved me, as you told me so. A feeling of euphoria engulfed my whole being, but you told me that you were divorced, I felt happy, then you said you were married again, and then I sank and was fearful.

I was always aware of that fact, and kept reminding you. You said "I take full responsibility for everything I do." There was great difficulty in keeping our love from each other, so we did not, because we could not.

For almost ten years we talked to each other almost every day for hours at a time. We loved, we quarrelled, we made up, and we saw each other. You told me you wanted to be with me, you told me you wanted to marry me and spend the rest of your life with me, that we would be so happy together. Once again, you knew what you wanted, once again, I knew what I wanted, and that was just to be with you. I did not want material things from you, I just wanted to share what I had with you and as long as we had a roof over our heads, and food on our table so we could share with others, I would be happy as that was all I wanted, and I would be so happy taking care of you.

Once again, you knew what you wanted, but did not know how to make a decision to get it. Again, I made myself available and was very vulnerable, but once again you did not know how to make the right decision on how to get what you wanted. Remember, I was alone, and I waited, you asked me to. You were lonely, your children were grown up and married with children of their own, so were mine. Thank God, I never did hide anything from my children.

You were unhappy in the situation in which you found yourself due to wrong and uncomfortable decisions you made, which you knew were wrong, this I know, because you started looking for me again, shortly after, and here I was alone for eight years. I know, you try to blame me, but because I know you so well, you try not to take responsibility for the things you did that affected both our lives. I am so sorry for all the unhappiness you suffered, for the decisions we both made, all I ever wanted to do was to love you, love you, love you and take care of you. No one knew you as much and as well as I knew you.

As I have said so many times to you, Deiter, I do love you, but it was very painful to love you, as when you believed you were vulnerable, you tried to deflect your vulnerability, but that did not deter me, because I knew you loved me with an everlasting love, because I felt it, and when you tried to camouflage it, I made you know, and you were right back to me. It was also so very easy to love you, as with me your love knew no bounds. You have said that you do not know, anymore, what love is, I say "phew" to that, you do know, as I have felt its depth from you, in your actions and your embrace. I have it, and I have always kept it aglow in my heart. You also said that you had given me all your love, every ounce of it, and you could not take it back. Thanks, because I have it and will always cherish it, as you have had all and every ounce of mine.

You have also told me that I was the only person in this world that knows the softer side of you. I don't know any other side. As that is the only side I know, and I thank you for that, and I thank you for your love. I am eternally grateful for that, for all the joy, laughter, quarrels, rudeness, arguments and most of all the joy and happiness you brought into my life. God makes no mistakes, He knew why He brought us together, as we shared so much laughter together. I just loved it when you laughed.

I am also eternally grateful for the very last conversation we had, you wanted me there with you. You just wanted to sit and do nothing. You said we would do nothing together, and we would be so happy together. You sang to me, we laughed a lot together, we talked of our love, we talked for about an hour and a half, and within less than an hour after, you were gone, as God took you home.

My dearest, our love is eternal, there is more for us to do, and we will be together again. This time forever, as one.

All my love,
Yours forever,
Marcey.

Sleep well my love, sleep well.

About the Author

The author is a Social Worker and a Career Consultant with an interesting love life. She was married for over Thirty Years to a wonderful man who was suddenly taken from her. Years after his passing, her first love returned to her life. She is retired and can now reflect with both happiness and sadness as she shares her story, and further looks forward towards a life of peace and contentment.